PENGUIN BOOKS

DISTRUST THAT PARTICULAR FLAVOR

William Gibson's first novel *Neuromancer* has sold more than six million copies worldwide. In an earlier short story he had invented the term 'cyberspace'; a concept he developed in the novel, creating an iconography for the Information Age long before the spread of the Internet. His book won three major literary prizes. *Count Zero* and *Mona Lisa Overdrive* completed his first trilogy.

His other novels are *Virtual Light, Idoru* and *All Tomorrow's Parties* (which make up the Bridge trilogy); *Pattern Recognition, Spook Country, Zero History* and most recently *The Peripheral*. According to the *Guardian*, in terms of influence, he is 'probably the most important novelist of the past two decades'.

William Gibson was born in South Carolina, USA, but has lived in Vancouver, Canada, for many years.

D0528758

DISTRUST THAT PARTICULAR FLAVOR

WILLIAM GIBSON

PENGUIN BOOKS

PENGUIN BOOKS

Published by the Penguin Group
Penguin Books Ltd, 80 Strand, London WC2R ORL, England
Penguin Group (USA) Inc., 375 Hudson Street, New York, New York 10014, USA
Penguin Group (Canada), 90 Eglinton Avenue East, Suite 700, Toronto, Ontario, Canada M4P 2Y3
(a division of Pearson Penguin Canada Inc.)
Penguin Ireland, 25 St Stephen's Green, Dublin 2, Ireland (a division of Penguin Books Ltd)
Penguin Group (Australia), 707 Collins Street, Melbourne, Victoria 3008, Australia
(a division of Pearson Australia Group Pty Ltd)
Penguin Books India Pvt Ltd, 11 Community Centre, Panchsheel Park, New Delhi – 110 017, India
Penguin Group (NZ), 67 Apollo Drive, Rosedale, Auckland 0632, New Zealand
(a division of Pearson New Zealand Ltd)
Penguin Books (South Africa) (Pty) Ltd, Block D, Rosebank Office Park,
181 Jan Smuts Avenue, Parktown North, Gauteng 2193, South Africa

Penguin Books Ltd, Registered Offices: 80 Strand, London WC2R ORL, England

www.penguin.com

First published in the United States of America by G. P. Putnam's Sons 2012
First published in Great Britain by Viking 2012
Published in Penguin Books 2014

001

Copyright © William Gibson Ent. Ltd., 2012
All rights reserved

The moral right of the author has been asserted

The Credits on p. 257–9 constitute an extension of this copyright page

Photograph on facing page courtesy of Calvin Greenwood

Typeset by Jouve (UK), Milton Keynes
Printed in Great Britain by Clays Ltd, St Ives plc

Except in the United States of America, this book is sold subject
to the condition that it shall not, by way of trade or otherwise, be lent,
re-sold, hired out, or otherwise circulated without the publisher's
prior consent in any form of binding or cover other than that in
which it is published and without a similar condition including this
condition being imposed on the subsequent purchaser

ISBN: 978-0-241-96098-1

www.greenpenguin.co.uk

MIX
Paper from
responsible sources
FSC **FSC™ C018179**
www.fsc.org

Penguin Books is committed to a sustainable
future for our business, our readers and our planet.
This book is made from Forest Stewardship
Council™ certified paper.

CONTENTS

DISTRUST THAT PARTICULAR FLAVOR

INTRODUCTION:
AFRICAN THUMB PIANO

When I started to try to learn to write fiction, I knew that I had no idea how to write fiction. This was actually a plus, that I knew I didn't know, but at the time it was scary. I was afraid that people who were somehow destined to write fiction came to the task already knowing how. I clearly didn't, so likely I wasn't so destined. I sat at the typewriter, the one on which I'd written undergraduate essays, trying to figure out how to try.

Eventually I began to try to write a sentence. I tried to write it for months. It grew longer. Eventually it became: "Seated each afternoon in the darkened screening room, Graham came gradually to see the targeted numerals of the academy leader as hypnagogic sigils preceding the dreamstate of film." I'm not sure it was Graham. Maybe it was Bannister. It was a sentence far too obviously in the manner of J. G. Ballard, and Ballard gave his protagonists sturdy, everyman British middle-class surnames.

I had no idea what my sentence meant, in terms of where any narrative might go, but I now know that that was not a bad thing. I was in the first place of fiction, as was my protagonist. A door was opening, however slightly. I began to imagine that the deserted (recently deserted?) office building in which Graham/Bannister reviewed film had a fountain in its atrium, and in this fountain, submerged, along with the usual coins, were dozens of wristwatches, some of them very expensive. Time had ended, perhaps, or the awareness of its passage had become somehow undesirable. And that was as far as I went, the door closing. I may have sensed, correctly, that a Ballard pastiche, no matter how earnest, was somehow not the thing.

Later attempts sometimes involved outer space, though outer space more in the manner, I hoped, of Alfred Bester or Samuel R. Delany. I don't remember them. My wife parodied them all, not unkindly, as "His long green ears quivering, Fimo slipped from the rig." Today this reminds me that I was having trouble with character names. At one point I seriously considered borrowing them from products in the IKEA catalog. But there was always something akin to "the rig." Some unimagined (by me), hence unnamed, element of technology. But already I sensed that even if I had somehow come to know what the rig was, what it was for, it was better not to tell the reader just then. "Javnaker slipped from the quantum universe-splitter that wasn't actually a time machine" would not be good for the reader.

And therein, I think, lies most of how one learns to write fiction. We have to learn to write fiction, but we have already, to varying degrees, had to learn to read it. And I felt like quite a good reader of fiction, when I began to write fiction, or at least a good reader of that fiction which I most keenly enjoyed. And thus are we shaped as writers, I believe, not so much by who our favorite writers are as by our general experience of fiction. Learning to write fiction, we learn to listen for our own acquired sense of what feels right, based on the totality of the pleasure (or its lack) that fiction has provided us. Not direct emulation, but rather a matter of a personal micro-culture.

Knowing how seriously aspiring writers of fiction can take advice from more established writers of fiction, I'm generally reluctant to say more than: If you wish to learn to write fiction, it helps if you've read a lot of it before you begin to try. And that in any case, you'll likely need to spend a lot of time discovering how to try, and then a lot more time trying. I don't really remember anything very specific about learning to drive, other than a neat trick for parallel parking, and learning to write fiction is a lot like that (except for no terrified instructor in the passenger seat, though in a way we each provide one of those as well).

Eventually, I was able to write something like a story, and it was published, however obscurely. Later, after what seemed like dozens of false starts, I wrote several more. I began to meet other people who were attempting to write science fiction, and noticed that most of them had found ways to write, and to be read, that didn't involve payment. Science fiction had long been surrounded by a generations-deep compost of fanzines, a sort of paper Internet, and this could be extremely engrossing, and apparently gratifying. But after trying that avenue of publication a few times, I decided to avoid it.

My decision, such as it was, ran something like this: I am in the process of discovering that place from which my fiction comes, and the process may best be served by limiting the act of writing to the writing of fiction which I might reasonably expect to sell. (I don't offer this by way of advice, though, because some writers clearly thrive on exactly the opposite path.)

The distinction I was making wasn't between paid versus unpaid, exactly. It wasn't about whatever sum might be involved. It was about a certain demonstration of agency. It involved a harsher dichotomy. Every word written (or written then subtracted, which is often more important) contributed to the possibility, or not, of an event happening in the world outside oneself. Either someone whose rent was paid by their job of selecting stories, someone for whom it actually mattered, could be induced by my words on a page to buy my story, or they couldn't. This seemed like magic to me, and still does. As if the right runes, scratched in the dirt, could produce a bag of groceries. Once you've managed to do this successfully, doing it again isn't quite so much about the groceries as about the peculiar wonder of it.

The door into fiction-writing space began to open more easily, and more regularly. A huge amount of the thing is simply practice, but that practice, for me, had to be practice in the actual writing of fiction. The itch to become a writer could be scratched, I suspected, too easily, with other kinds of writing. Self-discipline never having been my strong suit, I became uncharacteristically strict with myself about writing only fiction.

Which is why I have never felt entirely comfortable with the pieces collected here.

They are violations of that early prime directive. They aren't fiction. Worse, they somehow aren't quite nonfiction either, it feels to me, because they were written from the fiction-writing place, the only writing place I had, with fiction-writing tools, the only writing tools I had. I didn't feel adequately professional, writing nonfiction. I felt as though I was being paid to solo on some instrument vaguely related to one I actually knew how to play.

I had had no formal training in journalism. The idea of keeping a diary or journal had always made me uncomfortable. The idea of direct, unfiltered autobiography made me even more uncomfortable. By the time I began to occasionally be asked to write nonfiction, the membrane surrounding the fiction-writing place had been sanded to a workable thinness, was porous. The world washed in, if I was lucky, and was transformed. On a good working day, I watched as some largely unconscious process turned reality, or what passed for it, into fantasy. Which was what I had wanted, how I had wanted to make my living. To write nonfiction felt worryingly counter to that.

And yet. Opportunities to visit new places, to meet interesting people. A certain permission to ask questions. These things can prove extraordinarily valuable to a writer of fiction. The peculiarity quotient of the stuff washing in through the membrane rises. One is in Tokyo, one is in Singapore, one is in the Zona Rosa or in an after-hours club in Dublin. And someone else is paying for it. Is paying for you to be exactly there, doing approximately that, and the fiction-writing place, though you don't notice it at the time, benefits.

The lure of that got me out there, doing something I secretly felt I probably shouldn't quite be doing. The results are collected here, along with some "talks," an even more problematic form for me, because writers, it seems to me, should write, not make speeches. But speeches, like quasi-journalistic writing assignments, can come attached to plane tickets, to hotel rooms in cities one might never have thought of visiting otherwise. In writing speeches, curiously, one sometimes finds out what one thinks, at that moment, about something. The world at large, say. Or futurity. Or the impossibility of absolutely grasping either. Generally they make me even more uncomfortable to write than articles, but later, back in the place of writing fiction, I often discover that I have been trying to tell myself something.

When I taught myself to write fiction, I eventually accepted that I had learned to do what passes for the writing of fiction when I'm the one doing it. The volume on the imposter-syndrome module decreased. Writing nonfiction, I've often felt as though I'm applying latex paint to the living room walls with a toothbrush. The volume on the module shoots up. Perhaps people will assume that the resulting texture is deliberate. Perhaps not. Writing fiction is a unique activity for me, a neurological territory, an altered state. Writing nonfiction isn't, quite, but I'm gradually coming to accept that I've learned to do what passes for the writing of nonfiction when I'm the one doing it.

The following pieces are performed, then, on the African thumb piano, an instrument I scarcely know how to play.

They were composed, however, on one that has no name, and which I am yet to see.

—VANCOUVER, AUGUST 2011

ROCKET RADIO

ROLLING STONE

JUNE 1989

THE BOY CROUCHES beside a fence in Virginia, listening to Chubby Checker on the Rocket Radio. The fence is iron, very old, unpainted, its uprights shaved down by rain and the steady turning of seasons. The Rocket Radio is red plastic, fastened to the fence with an alligator clip. Chubby Checker sings into the boy's ear through a plastic plug. The wires that connect the plug and the clip to the Rocket Radio are the color his model kits call "flesh." The Rocket Radio is something he can hide in his palm. His mother says the Rocket Radio is a crystal radio: She says she remembers boys building them before you could buy them, to catch the signals spilling out of the sky.

The Rocket Radio requires no battery at all. Uses a quarter mile of neighbor's rusting fence for an antenna.

Chubby Checker says do the twist.

The boy with the Rocket Radio reads a lot of science fiction— very little of which will help to prepare him for the coming re- alities of the Net.

He doesn't even know that Chubby Checker and the Rocket Radio are part of the Net.

———

ONCE PERFECTED, communication technologies rarely die out entirely; rather, they shrink to fit particular niches in the global info-structure. Crystal radios have been proposed as a means of conveying optimal seed-planting times to isolated agrarian tribes. The mimeograph, one of many recent dinosaurs of the urban office place, still shines with undiminished samizdat potential in the century's backwaters, the late-Victorian answer to desktop publishing. Banks in uncounted third-world villages still crank the day's totals on black Burroughs adding machines, spooling out yards of faint indigo figures on long, oddly festive curls of paper, while the Soviet Union, not yet sold on throwaway new-tech fun, has become the last reliable source of vacuum tubes. The eight-track–tape format survives in the truck stops of the Deep South, as a medium for country music and spoken-word pornography.

The Street finds its own uses for things—uses the manufacturers never imagined. The microcassette recorder, originally intended for on-the-jump executive dictation, becomes the revolutionary medium of *magnitizdat*, allowing the covert spread of suppressed political speeches in Poland and China. The beeper and the cellular telephone become tools in an increasingly competitive market in illicit drugs. Other technological artifacts unexpectedly become means of communication, either through opportunity or necessity. The aerosol can gives birth to the urban graffiti matrix. Soviet rockers press homemade flexi-discs out of used chest X rays.

THE KID with the Rocket Radio gets older. One day he discovers sixty feet of weirdly skinny magnetic tape snarled in roadside Ontario brush. This is toward the end of the Eight-Track Era. He deduces the existence of the new and exotic cassette format: this semi-alien substance, jettisoned in frustration from the smooth hull of some hurtling 'Vette, settling like new-tech angel hair.

I BELONG to a generation of Americans who dimly recall the world prior to television. Many of us, I suspect, feel vaguely ashamed about this, as though the world before television was not quite, well, the world. The world before television equates with the world before the Net—the mass culture and the mechanisms of Information. And we are of the Net; to recall another mode of being is to admit to having once been something other than human.

The Net, in our lifetime, has propagated itself with viral rapidity, and continues to do so.

In Japan, where so many of the Net's components are developed and manufactured, this frantic evolution of form has been embraced with unequaled enthusiasm. Akihabara, Tokyo's vast retail electronics market, vibrates with a constant hum of biz in a city where antiquated three-year-old Trinitrons regularly find their way into landfill. But even in Tokyo one finds a reassuring degree of Net-induced transitional anxiety, as I learned when I met Katsuhiro Otomo, creator of Akira, a vastly popular multivolume graphic novel. Neither of us spoke the other's language: Our mutual publisher had supplied a translator, and our "conversation" was relentlessly documented. But Otomo and I were still able to share a moment of universal techno-angst.

HIS LIVING ROOM was dominated by a vast matte-black media node that would put most Hollywood producers to shame. He pointed to an eight-inch stack of remote-control devices.

"I don't know how to use them," he said, "but my children do."

"I don't know how to use mine, either."

Otomo laughed.

Today, Otomo's collection of remotes is probably part of some artfully bulldozed *gomi* plain, landfill for Neo-Tokyo. *Gomi*: Japanese for "garbage," a lot of which consists of outmoded consumer electronics—such as those recently redundant remotes. Wisely assuming a constant source, the Japanese build themselves more island out of it.

The sexiness of newness, and how it wears thin. The metaphysics of consumer desire, in these final years of the twentieth century . . .

Two years ago I was finally shamed into acquiring a decent audio system. A friend had turned up in the new guise of high-end-audio importer, and my old "system," so to speak, caused him actual pain. He offered to go wholesale on a total package, provided I let him select the bits and pieces.

I did.

It sounds fine.

But I'm not sure I really enjoy the music any more than I did before, on certifiably low-fi junk. The music, when it's really there, is just there. You can hear it coming out of the dented speaker grille of a Datsun B210 with holes in the floor. Sometimes that's the best way to hear it.

I knew a man once whose teen years had been L.A., jazz, the Forties. He spoke of afternoons he'd spent, utterly transported, playing 78-rpm recordings, "worn down white" with repeated applications of a sharp steel stylus. That is, the shellac that carried the grooves on these originally black records was plain gone: What he must have been listening to could only have been the faintest approximations of the original sound. (Rationing affected steel phonograph needles, he told me, desperate hipsters resorted to the spikes of the larger cactuses.)

That man heard that music.

I first heard the Rolling Stones on a battery-powered, basketball-shaped, pigskin-covered miniature phonograph of French manufacture—a piece of low tech as radical in its day as it is now obscure. Radical in that it enabled the teenage owner to transport LP records and the intoxicant of choice to suitably private locations—the boonies.

This constituted an entirely new way to listen to the music of choice. "Choice" being the key word. The revolutionary potential of the D-cell record player wasn't substantially bettered until the advent of the Walkman, which allows us to integrate the music of choice with virtually any landscape.

The Walkman changed the way we understand cities.

I first heard Joy Division on a Walkman, and I remain unable to separate the experience of the music's bleak majesty from the first heady discovery of the pleasures of musically encapsulated fast-forward urban motion.

In the Seventies, the Net writhed with growth. Gaps began to close. A paradox became increasingly evident: While artists needed the Net in order to reach a mass audience, it seemed to be the gaps through which the best art emerged, at least initially.

I am, by trade, a science-fiction writer. That is, the fiction I've written so far has arrived at the point of consumption via a marketing mechanism called "science fiction." During the past twenty years the Net has closed around mass-market publishing—and science fiction—as smoothly as it closed around the music industry and everything else.

As a science-fiction writer, I'm sometimes asked whether or not I think the Net is a good thing. That's like being asked if being human is a good thing. As for being a human being a good thing or not, I can't say—this has been referred to as the Post-modern Condition.

In any case it sometimes looks to me as though lots of us will eventually have a basis for comparison, by virtue of no longer being quite human at all, thank you.

Meanwhile, in my front room, the family media node is in metastasis, sprouting CDs, joysticks, you name it. My kids, like Mr. Otomo's, cluster like flies.

THE OTHER THING they ask you when you're a science-fiction writer is, "What do you think will happen?"

The day I reply with anything other than a qualified "I haven't got a clue," please shoot me. While science fiction is sometimes good at predicting things, it's seldom good at predicting what those things might actually do to us. For example, television, staple window dressing for hundreds of stories from the Twenties through the Forties, was usually presented as a mode of personal communication. Nobody predicted commercials, *Hollywood Squares*, or heavy-metal music videos.

With that disclaimer firmly in place, I predict the family media node growing into a trickier and more unified lump. The distinction among television, CD player, and computer seems particularly arbitrary these days, a tired scam designed to support the robots who solder circuit boards. But as to what your integrated Net Node will actually be able to do for you one day, my best bet is that the words for it haven't been invented yet.

Example. A BBC executive working on another vision of "interactive television" offered me a tour of a small research facility in San Francisco. He was interested in having me "do" something with this new technology: The lab we visited was devoted to ... well, there weren't verbs. I looked at things, watched consoles as they were poked and prodded, and nobody there, it seemed, could even begin to explain what it was I might be doing if I were to, uh, do one of these projects, whatever it was. It wasn't writing, and it wasn't directing. It was definitely something, though, and they were certainly keen to do it, but they needed those verbs.

Another example. A week later I found myself in an FX compound situated off a quiet back street in North Hollywood, experiencing serious future-shock frisson. My hosts—young, fast, and scientific to the bone—had developed a real-time video puppet, a slack-faced Max Headroom suspended in the imaginary space behind a television screen. Invited to put my hand in a waldo that looked vaguely like a gyroscope, I caused this sleeping golem to twitch and shiver, and my own hair to stand on end. On the way out, I was given a tape of the thing being manipulated by a professional movie puppeteer. It looks a lot more natural than I ever do on television, but what are the verbs for what those young fast fellows were doing?

We hurtle toward an imaginary vortex, the century's end. . . .

HE GETS UP in the morning and watches ten minutes of Much-Music while the water boils for coffee. The kids aren't up yet because it's not quite time for *Dinosaurs*. MuchMusic is Canada's approximation of MTV. In the morning he usually watches it with the sound off, unless they show a video from Quebec, in which case he listens because he doesn't understand French.

Because he doesn't like the Net to gnaw at the remnants of the night's dreams. Not until he's ready for it to anyway.

These pieces aren't presented in chronological order, particularly, but this is quite an early example, and the product of considerable discomfort around the idea of just how one does this sort of thing when asked. The very fact of the commission was unsettling, I recall.

What I don't recall, quite, is what I would have imagined "the Net" to be, at that point, however freely I tossed the term around for Rolling Stone. *I knew not Net, when I wrote this, though I had friends who talked Net, and fairly constantly. I communicated with them via fax, yards and yards of slippery, oddly scented photosensitive paper, longer docs coming or going via FedEx, either as printouts or on floppies. So I think it's safe to say that I was pretending to know what "the Net" might be, when I wrote this. Was it something to do with this "email" a few people seemed to know how to send between distant computers, or was it some more abstract expression of the totality of cyberspace? I think I opted for the latter, but phrased things in such a way as might seem I was better acquainted with the former than I actually was.*

If I had seen a computer with an Internet connection, at that point, I hadn't been aware of it. The first I remember seeing was my own, and that was quite a few years later; I'd waited until they'd made it very simple, which I'd rightly assumed they would, eventually.

But I did own a Rocket Radio when I was a kid, and I did once infer the existence of the newfangled tape cassette from a single brown and tangled roadside skein.

The Datsun B-210 with rust-holes in the floor was my own, parked outside as I wrote.

SINCE 1948

AUTOBIOGRAPHY FOR THE AUTHOR'S WEBSITE

NOVEMBER 2002

GENE WOLFE ONCE said that being an only child whose parents are dead is like being the sole survivor of drowned Atlantis. There was a whole civilization there, an entire continent, but it's gone. And you alone remember. That's my story too, my father having died when I was six, my mother when I was eighteen. Brian Aldiss believes that if you look at the life of any novelist, you'll find an early traumatic break, and mine seems no exception.

I was born on the coast of South Carolina, where my parents liked to vacation when there was almost nothing there at all. My father was in some sort of middle-management position in a large and growing construction company. They'd built some of the Oak Ridge atomic facilities, and paranoiac legends of "security" at Oak Ridge were part of our family culture. There was a cigar box full of strange-looking ID badges he'd worn there. But he'd done well at Oak Ridge, evidently, and so had the company he worked for, and in the postwar South they were busy building entire red brick Levittown-style suburbs. We moved a lot, following these projects, and he was frequently away, scouting for new ones.

It was a world of early television, a new Oldsmobile with

crazy rocket-ship styling, toys with science-fiction themes. Then my father went off on one more business trip. He never came back. He choked on something in a restaurant, the Heimlich maneuver hadn't been discovered yet, and everything changed.

My mother took me back to the small town in southwestern Virginia where both she and my father were from, a place where modernity had arrived to some extent but was deeply distrusted. The trauma of my father's death aside, I'm convinced that it was this experience of feeling abruptly exiled, to what seemed like the past, that began my relationship with science fiction.

I eventually became exactly the sort of introverted, hyper-bookish boy you'll find in the biographies of most American science-fiction writers, obsessively filling shelves with paperbacks and digest-sized magazines, dreaming of one day becoming a writer myself.

At age fifteen, my chronically anxious and depressive mother having demonstrated an uncharacteristic burst of common sense in what today we call "parenting," I was shipped off to a private boys' school in Arizona. There, extracted grublike and blinking from my bedroom and those bulging plywood shelves, I began the forced invention of a less Lovecraftian persona—based in large part on a chance literary discovery a year or so before.

I had stumbled, in my ceaseless quest for more and/or better science fiction, on a writer named Burroughs—not Edgar Rice but William S., and with him had come his colleagues Kerouac and Ginsberg. I had read this stuff, or tried to, with no idea at all of what it might mean, and felt compelled—compelled to what, I didn't know. The effect, over the next few years, was to make me, at least in terms of my Virginia home, Patient Zero of what would later be called the counterculture. At the time, I had no way of knowing that millions of other boomer babes, changelings all, were undergoing the same metamorphosis.

In Arizona, science fiction was put aside with other childish things, as I set about negotiating puberty and trying on alternate personae with all the urgency and clumsiness that come with that, and was actually getting somewhere, I think, when my mother died with stunning suddenness. Dropped literally dead: the descent of an Other Shoe I'd been anticipating since age six.

Thereafter, probably needless to say, things didn't seem to go very well for quite a while. I left my school without graduating, joined up with the rest of the Children's Crusade of the day, and shortly found myself in Canada, a country I knew almost nothing about. I concentrated on evading the draft and staying alive, while trying to make sure I looked like I was at least enjoying the Summer of Love. I did literally evade the draft, as they never bothered drafting me, and have lived here in Canada, more or less, ever since.

Having ridden out the crest of the Sixties in Toronto, aside from a brief, riot-torn spell in the District of Columbia, I met a girl from Vancouver, went off to Europe with her (concentrating on countries with fascist regimes and highly favorable rates of exchange), got married, and moved to British Columbia, where I watched the hot fat of the Sixties congeal as I earned a desultory bachelor's degree in English at UBC.

In 1977, facing first-time parenthood and an absolute lack of enthusiasm for anything like "career," I found myself dusting off my twelve-year-old's interest in science fiction. Simultaneously, weird noises were being heard from New York and London. I took Punk to be the detonation of some slow-fused projectile buried deep in society's flank a decade earlier, and I took it to be, somehow, a sign. And I began, then, to write.

And have been, ever since.

Google me and you can learn that I do it all on a manual typewriter, something that hasn't been true since 1985, but which makes such an easy hook for a lazy journalist that I expect to be reading it for the rest of my life. I only used a typewriter because that was what everyone used in 1977, and it was manual because that was what I happened to have been able to get, for free. I did avoid the Internet, but only until the advent of the Web turned it into such a magnificent opportunity to waste time that I could no longer resist. Today I probably spend as much time there as I do anywhere, although the really peculiar thing about me, demographically, is that I probably watch less than twelve hours of television in a given year, and have watched that little since age fifteen. (An individual who watches no television is still a scarcer beast than one who doesn't have an e-mail address.) I have no idea how that happened. It wasn't a decision.

I do have an e-mail address, yes, but, no, I won't give it to you. I am one and you are many, and even if you are, say, twenty-seven in grand global total, that's still too many. Because I need to have a life and waste time and write.

I suspect I have spent just about exactly as much time actually

writing as the average person my age has spent watching television, and that, as much as anything, may be the real secret here.

I wrote this when Penguin USA was setting up a website for
me. I'm sure they suggested it, but fortunately it didn't trigger
any of that commission-by-a-major-publication adrenaline.

I now spend at least as much time on the Internet as the
average person used to spend watching television. But I still
watch very little television in the conventional, or previous,
sense.

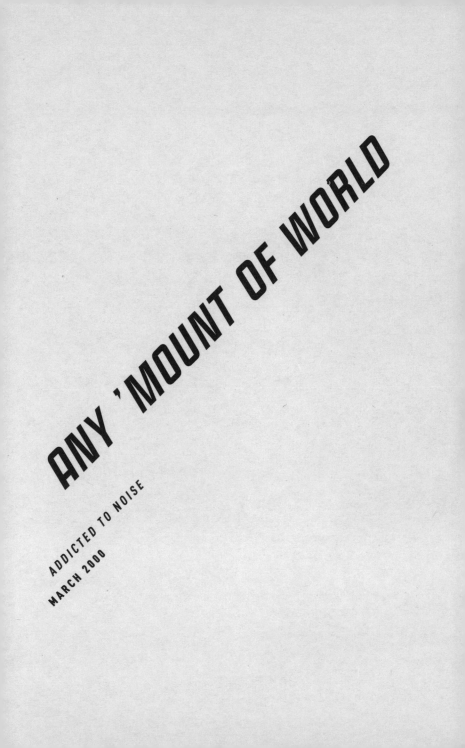

ANY 'MOUNT OF WORLD

ADDICTED TO NOISE

MARCH 2000

ARTISTIC COLLABORATION IS A PROFOUNDLY strange business. Do it right up to the hilt, as it were, and you and your partner will generate a third party, some thoroughly Other, and often one capable of things neither you nor the very reasonable gentleman seated opposite would even begin to consider. "Who," asks one of those disembodied voices in Mr. Burroughs's multilevel scrapbooks, "is the Third who walks beside us?"

My theory, such as it is, about Walter Becker and Donald Fagen, is that their Third, their Other, Mistah Steely Dan hisself, proved so problematic an entity for the both of them, so seductive and determined a swirl of ectoplasm, that they opted to stay the hell away from him for twenty years.

He continues on, of course, in the atemporal reaches of electronic popular culture, and I have often raised an eyebrow at hearing him sing, as I push a cart down some Safeway aisle, of the spiritual complexities induced by the admixture of Cuervo Gold, cocaine, and nineteen-year-old girls (in the hands of a man of, shall we say, a certain age). At which point I look around Frozen Foods and wonder: "Is anyone else hearing this?" Do the people who program these supermarket background tapes have any idea what this song is actually about? On this basis alone I have always maintained that Steely Dan's music was, has been, and remains among the most genuinely subversive oeuvres in late-twentieth-century pop.

There's a story about some hapless mook, down under the stadium there in Chicago where they did the hands-on prep for the first atomic bomb, who finds himself in the deeply unenviable position of having to shove together two halves of some grapefruit-sized mass of critically radioactive material. It ends, as they say, in tears, and that is what I've always imagined happened to Becker and Fagen; why they opted offshore and waited a couple of decades for the Geiger counters to stop clicking. Buried the two halves of that graphite core under their respective beds, maybe never to be reassembled.

Now whatever Mistah Dan might be—and I myself am inclined to think of him as a literary, or perhaps paraliterary, as much as a purely musical figure—Becker and Fagen are musos of the first water. Hence their respective solo output in the absence of Steely Dan. Which I've enjoyed, but in rather an oblique way, never quite able to stop glancing over my shoulder else that Third might loom suddenly into view, which he never did.

Now comes, as surely every Dan fan knows, *Two Against Nature*. The immediate and embarrassingly looming question being: Is He back? Have they resurrected His Bad Self?

Yes.

They have. The Stranger has signed in, his toe-cleavage ostrich loafers flaking red Maui clay on the studio broadloom.

Two Against Nature is actually a rather eerie experience in that regard, like being present for the arrival of a time machine. But not one from any particular past, or future; this music manages (as it always has) to transcend the duller registers of the cultural calendar. It's as though it was composed in the time machine, in its own little pocket of temporality. I suspect that this is somehow the result of an encyclopedic sense of American music, an effortlessly graceful facility at collage and that patented Steely Dan studio wax, as though one were listening down through a hundred coats of hand-rubbed sonic carnauba, each glossy layer somehow highlighting a different aspect of the composition. But best ignore that, as I am anything but a musician. Suffice it to say: It sure sounds like Steely Dan to me, and the more so the longer I listen to it.

The DNA match is perfect. The real question, I think, is how close together have Becker and Fagen been willing to bring the two halves of the graphite core? Well, sometimes very close, it feels to me, and sometimes not so. My Dan counter starts to sizzle most seriously with "Jack of Speed" and "Cousin Dupree," two very different pieces. "Jack of Speed" is an instant classic in the Dan Archive of Loping Psychedelic Naturalism, one of those luminously unfocused mug shots they're so good at: Someone you once knew all too well, shuffled back, via the Dan magic, to stand in your doorway for a moment with Orphan Annie eyes. "Cousin Dupree" is Steely Dan at the very peak of droll American pop narrative, deeply comic and quietly merciless.

I'd say more about the other songs, but I'm starting to feel like a reviewer, which makes me intensely uncomfortable. I'm not a reviewer: I just want to say I like this record a lot, okay?

And I can only hope that Becker and Fagen decide that they can afford to let their Third out of the box a little more often, as there's nobody else remotely like him, and we need him. I know I do.

One of the more peculiar, more semiconscious exercises I practiced, early in my fiction-writing career, consisted of reading record reviews in, say, Melody Maker, *while pretending that I was actually reading a review of a new science fiction novel. I would later attempt to recall that novel, my sense of it from the review, as a species of writing-prompt.*

Steely Dan's recordings had never required that extra step, as I had from very first listening assumed them to be producing a remarkable species of narrative fiction. The popularity of their music, back when, had amazed me, as anything I liked that much wasn't supposed to be that popular. I assumed that that was because most listeners scarcely brushed against the complexly strung razor-wire of the lyrics, dressed as they were in Kandy Apple jazzgloss. Becker and Fagen remain, most days, my favorite twentieth-century lyricists, to the frank dismay of friends in the Punk camp, who absolutely don't get it. Never mind. We find it where we find it, inspira-tionwise.

Over a decade after I wrote this, it was my very great plea-sure to get to know Mr. Becker somewhat, and to meet Mr. Fagen all too briefly. Never have my culture-heroes proven less disappointing.

THE BADDEST
DUDE ON EARTH

TIME ASIA
APRIL 2002

I ONCE WROTE A SCREENPLAY which featured a stoical, traditionalist *Yakuza* boss, exiled, in my near-future scenario, to the frozen, cockroach-ridden wastes of a dystopian Newark, New Jersey. Clenched like a fist around his grief at the loss of his daughter, he soldiers on, like a Roman legionary with a death wish the size of a Volkswagen on his shoulder. Meanwhile, his decadent, hotshot young understudy, a bio-tech dandy with a lethal thumb implant, watches for the earliest, easiest opportunity to kill him.

Where, I now wonder, did I find this character, this hard, immaculate man with his hidden inner wound? I had not, at that time, seen any *Yakuza* films, although I was aware of the genre by some species of pop-culture osmosis. And I had sensed that the roots of that genre would somehow be tangled in a rich mulch of American westerns and gangster films. I was somehow aware of the character as a re-importation. As a friend likes to say, there's often something in a good translation that can't quite be captured in the original. But where did my tough and tragic *Yakuza* boss come from?

He came, somehow, from the films of Takeshi Kitano, which I had not yet seen. He arrived as the crystalline, free-floating essence of an idea or stance. He owed everything to "Beat" Takeshi, a Japanese pop figure of such unstintingly multitalented eclecticism that we have no equivalent, nobody even close. ("They only want you to be the one thing," Mick Jagger once told me, speaking of his own acting career.) Writer, producer, director, actor, television personality, comedian . . . But I knew nothing of that, as I wrote. Nor could I know that Takeshi, whose gravitas would one day tug at the film with the pull of a black hole, was said to be both a very great actor and the most famous man in Japan. Both of which, now I know, were and are true.

Fast-forward to a vast, freezing, dilapidated factory building on the outskirts of Toronto, in which has been constructed a segment of my dystopian near-future Newark, an aerial shantytown slung beneath a bridge. Here, amid cameras and crew and the patchwork of our junkyard set, I watch Takeshi prepare to portray my *Yakuza* boss.

I'm terrified. I've only just seen, for the first time, the day before, actors portraying characters I've written. And now Takeshi strikes me as a *tulpa*, a materialized thought-form, sentient plasm of whatever cross-cultural meme generated this character through me. I don't believe he's acting. As if to reinforce this, his entourage of smooth-faced, unblinking young associates dress as if in imitation of his character's costume. Or, rather, as if they had no need for imitation, being already there. Like the character, they are all buttoned into beautifully cut cashmere overcoats. Black.

I never saw Takeshi again, and then, months later, I heard that he had been terribly injured in a motorcycle accident, and was at first not expected to live, and then, when he did live, was not expected to be able to act again.

It made me very sad.

I thought of all this, this past summer, as I watched his film *Brother* in the Vancouver Film Festival, one of the only films I've seen which captures the micron-thin veneer of city-over-desert that one sees constantly in the parts of Los Angeles one never sees in films. Takeshi had survived his motorcycle crash, with the newly limited mobility of his features turned to full advantage as he takes us on his character's somberly delirious kamikaze run into a simpler and more hauntingly realized vision of night-side America than our own directors have given us for quite a long time.

Toughness has been rather out of fashion, as a masculine virtue, and Takeshi simultaneously radiates it and suggests its wounded core. There can in fact be no depiction of genuine toughness (not brutality but a sort of excess of substance, of soul-stuff) without this concomitant indication of that wound, else the piece becomes simply the pornography of fascism.

Takeshi is simultaneously tougher and more wounded than you or I will ever be. Given the ever deeper and more precise reach of the spectral hand of marketing, I suspect that he's tougher and more wounded than any Hollywood star is ever likely to be allowed to be.

When I wrote this, I hadn't yet realized that Bruce Sterling, when he spoke of translations, was paraphrasing Jorge Luis Borges.

If you'd like to see a Takeshi Kitano film, I recommend Sonatine.

Johnny Mnemonic, *as cut for the film's Japanese release, is some minutes longer, all of that in the service of delivering more Takeshi Kitano, and is of course the better for it.*

TALK FOR BOOK EXPO, NEW YORK

MAY 2010

SAY IT'S MIDWAY through the final year of the first decade of the twenty-first century. Say that, last week, two things happened: Scientists in China announced successful quantum teleportation over a distance of ten miles, while other scientists, in Maryland, announced the creation of an artificial, self-replicating genome. In this particular version of the twenty-first century, which happens to be the one you're living in, neither of these stories attracted a very great deal of attention.

In quantum teleportation, no matter is transferred, but information may be conveyed across a distance, without resorting to a signal in any traditional sense. Still, it's the word "teleportation," used seriously, in a headline. My "no kidding" module was activated: "No kidding," I said to myself, "teleportation." A slight amazement.

The synthetic genome, arguably artificial life, was somehow less amazing. The sort of thing one feels might already have been achieved, somehow. Triggering the "Oh, yeah" module. "Artificial life? Oh, yeah."

Though these scientists also inserted a line of James Joyce's prose into their genome. That triggers a sense of the surreal, in me at least. They did it to incorporate a yardstick for the ongoing measurement of mutation. So James Joyce's prose is now being very slowly pummeled into incoherence by cosmic rays.

Noting these two pieces of more or less simultaneous news, I also noted that my imagination, which grew up on countless popular imaginings of exactly this sort of thing, could produce nothing better in response than a tabloid headline: SYNTHETIC BACTERIA IN QUANTUM FREE-SPACE TELEPORTATION SHOCKER.

Alvin Toffler warned us about Future Shock, but is this Future Fatigue? For the past decade or so, the only critics of science fiction I pay any attention to, all three of them, have been slyly declaring that the Future is over. I wouldn't blame anyone for assuming that this is akin to the declaration that history was over, and just as silly. But really I think they're talking about the capital-F Future, which in my lifetime has been a cult, if not a religion. People my age are products of the culture of the capital-F Future. The younger you are, the less you are a product of that. If you're fifteen or so, today, I suspect that you inhabit a sort of endless digital Now, a state of atemporality enabled by our increasingly efficient communal prosthetic memory. I also suspect that you don't know it, because, as anthropologists tell us, one cannot know one's own culture.

The Future, capital-F, be it crystalline city on the hill or radioactive postnuclear wasteland, is gone. Ahead of us, there is merely . . . more stuff. Events. Some tending to the crystalline, some to the wasteland-y. Stuff: the mixed bag of the quotidian.

Please don't mistake this for one of those "after us, the deluge" moments on my part. I've always found those appalling, and most particularly when uttered by aging futurists, who of all people should know better. This newfound state of No Future is, in my opinion, a very good thing. It indicates a kind of maturity, an understanding that every future is someone else's past, every present someone else's future. Upon arriving in the capital-F Future, we discover it, invariably, to be the lower-case now.

The best science fiction has always known that, but it was a sort of cultural secret. When I began to write fiction, at the very end of the Seventies, I was fortunate to have been taught, as an undergraduate, that imaginary futures are always, regardless of what the authors might think, about the day in which they're written. Orwell knew it, writing *Nineteen Eighty-Four* in 1948, and I knew it writing *Neuromancer*, my first novel, which was published in 1984.

Neuromancer, though it's careful never to admit it, is set in the 2030s, when there's something like the Internet, but called "cyberspace," and a complete absence of cell phones, which I'm sure young readers assume must be a key plot-point. More accurately, there's something like cyberspace, but called "cyberspace," but that gets confusing. I followed *Neuromancer* with two more novels set in that particular future, but by then I was growing frustrated with the capital-F Future. I knew that those books were actually about the 1980s, when they were written, but almost nobody else seemed to see that.

So I wrote a novel called *Virtual Light*, which was set in 2006, which was then the very near future, and followed it with two more novels, each set a few imaginary years later, in what was really my take on the 1990s. It didn't seem to make any difference. Lots of people assumed I was still writing about the capital-F future. I began to tell interviewers, somewhat testily, that I believed I could write a novel set in the present, our present, then, which would have exactly the affect of my supposed imaginary futures. Hadn't J. G. Ballard declared Earth to be the real alien planet? Wasn't the future now?

SO I DID. In 2001, I was writing a book that became *Pattern Recognition*, my seventh novel, though it only did so after 9-11, which I'm fairly certain will be the real start of every documentary ever to be made about the present century. I found the material of the actual twenty-first century richer, stranger, more multiplex, than any imaginary twenty-first century could ever have been. And it could be unpacked with the toolkit of science fiction. I don't really see how it can be unpacked otherwise, as so much of it is so utterly akin to science fiction, complete with a workaday level of cognitive dissonance we now take utterly for granted.

Zero History, my ninth novel, will be published this September, rounding out that third set of three books. It's set in London and Paris, last year, in the wake of global financial collapse.

I wish that I could tell you what it's about, but I haven't yet discovered my best likely story, about that. That will come with reviews, audience and bookseller feedback (and booksellers are especially helpful, in that way). Along with however many interviews, these things will serve as a sort of oracle, suggesting to me what it is I've been doing for the past couple of years.

If *Pattern Recognition* was about the immediate psychic aftermath of 9-11, and *Spook Country* about the deep end of the Bush administration and the invasion of Iraq, I could say that *Zero History* is about the global financial crisis as some sort of nodal event, but that must be true of any 2010 novel with ambitions on the 2010 zeitgeist. But all three of these novels are also about that dawning recognition that the future, be it capital-T Tomorrow or just tomorrow, Friday, just means more stuff, however peculiar and unexpected. A new quotidian. Somebody's future, somebody else's past.

Simply in terms of ingredients, it's about recent trends in the evolution of the psychology of luxury goods, crooked former Special Forces officers, corrupt military contractors, the wonderfully bizarre symbiotic relationship between designers of high-end snowboarding gear and manufacturers of military clothing, and the increasingly virtual nature of the global market.

I called it *Zero History* because one of the characters has had a missing decade, during which he paid no taxes and had no credit cards. He meets a federal agent, who tells him that that combination indicates to her that he hasn't been up to much good, the past ten years. But that quotidian now finds him. Events find him, and he starts to acquire a history. And, one assumes, a credit rating, and the need to pay taxes.

It's also the first book I've written in which anyone gets engaged to be married.

A book exists at the intersection of the author's subconscious and the reader's response. An author's career exists in the same way. A writer worries away at a jumble of thoughts, building them into a device that communicates, but the writer doesn't know what's been communicated until it's possible to see it communicated.

After thirty years, a writer looks back and sees a career of a certain shape, utterly unanticipated.

It's a mysterious business, the writing of fiction, and I thank you all for making it possible.

This was given (that is, read aloud with some minimal attempts at appropriate body language) at a box lunch event for booksellers at Book Expo, which used to be called the ABA, for American Booksellers Association, whose oceanic trade fair it is. It's a daunting experience for an author, Book Expo, if only in sheer scale of numbers. You've never seen so many new books, and one's own title the merest raindrop in that sea.

Sorry for the Zero History *pitch toward the end, but I had my marching orders.*

DEAD MAN SINGS

FORBES ASAP
NOVEMBER 1998

TIME MOVES IN ONE DIRECTION, memory in another.

We are that strange species that constructs artifacts intended to counter the natural flow of forgetting.

I sometimes think that nothing really is new; that the first pixels were particles of ocher clay, the bison rendered in just the resolution required. The bison still function perfectly, all these millennia later, and what screen in the world today shall we say that of in a decade? And yet the bison will be there for us, on whatever screens we have, carried out of the primal dark on some impulse we each have felt, as children, drawing. But carried nonetheless on this thing we have always been creating, this vast unlikely mechanism that carries memory in its interstices; this global, communal, prosthetic memory that we have been building since before we learned to build.

We live in, have lived through, a strange time. I know this because when I was a child, the flow of forgetting was relatively unimpeded. I know this because the dead were less of a constant presence, then. Because there was once no Rewind button. Because the soldiers dying in the Somme were black and white, and did not run as the living run. Because the world's attic was still untidy. Because there were old men in the mountain valleys of my Virginia childhood who remembered a time before recorded music.

When we turn on the radio in a New York hotel room and hear Elvis singing "Heartbreak Hotel," we are seldom struck by the peculiarity of our situation: that a dead man sings.

In the context of the longer life of the species, it is something that only just changed a moment ago. It is something new, and I sometimes feel that, yes, everything has changed. (This perpetual toggling between nothing being new, under the sun, and everything having very recently changed, absolutely, is perhaps the central driving tension of my work.)

Our "now" has become at once more unforgivingly brief and unprecedentedly elastic. The half-life of media product grows shorter still, till it threatens to vanish altogether, everything into some weird quantum logic of its own, the Warholian Fifteen Minutes becoming a quarklike blink. Yet once admitted to the culture's consensus pantheon, certain things seem destined to be with us for a very long time indeed. This is a function, in large part, of the Rewind button. And we would all of us, to some extent, wish to be in heavy rotation.

And as this capacity for recall (and recommodification) grows more universal, history itself is seen to be even more obviously a construct, subject to revision. If it has been our business, as a species, to dam the flow of time through the creation and maintenance of mechanisms of external memory, what will we become when all these mechanisms, as they now seem intended ultimately to do, merge?

The end-point of human culture may well be a single moment

of effectively endless duration, an infinite digital Now. But then, again, perhaps there is nothing new, in the end of all our beginnings, and the bison will be there, waiting for us.

I would like to take this opportunity to thank Forbes *(more properly the editors of* Forbes ASAP*) for inviting me to write basically anything at all, then not messing with it when I did. I have been mining this piece for over a decade now, most consciously for talks, less consciously but more constantly for fiction.*

It was entirely a matter of taking dictation from some part of my unconscious that rarely checks in this directly. I wish that that happened more frequently, but I'll take what I can get.

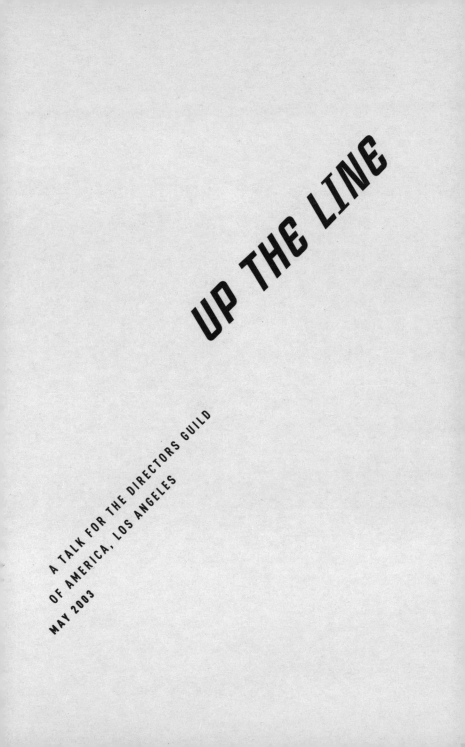

UP THE LINE

A TALK FOR THE DIRECTORS GUILD
OF AMERICA, LOS ANGELES
MAY 2003

THE STORY OF FILM begins around a fire, in darkness. Gathered around this fire are primates of a certain species, our ancestors, an animal distinguished by a peculiar ability to recognize patterns.

There is movement in the fire: embers glow and crawl on charcoal. Fire looks like nothing else. It generates light in darkness. It moves. It is alive.

The surrounding forest is dark. Is it the same forest our ancestors know by day? They can't be sure. At night it is another place. Without form, it is that on which our ancestors project the patterns their interestingly mutated brains generate.

This pattern-reading mutation is crucial to the survival of a species that must ceaselessly hunt, ceaselessly gather. One plant is good to eat; it grows in summer in these lowlands. But if you eat its seedpods, you sicken and die. The big, slow-moving river-animal can be surprised and killed, here in these shallows, but will escape in deeper water.

This function is already so central, in our ancestors, that they discover the outlines of the river-animal in clouds. They see the faces of wolves and of their own dead in the flames. They are already capable of symbolic thought. Spoken language is long since a fact for them but written language has not yet evolved. They scribe crisscross patterns on approximately rectangular bits of ocher, currently the world's oldest known human art.

They crouch, watching the fire, watching its constant, unpredictable movements, and someone is telling a story. In the watching of the fire and the telling of the tale lie the beginning of what we still call "film."

Later, on some other night, uncounted generations up the timeline, their descendants squat deep in caves, places of eternal night—painting. They paint by the less restless light of reeds and tallow. They paint the wolves and the river-animal, the gods and their dead. They have found ways to take control of certain aspects of the cooking-fire universe. Darkness lives here, in the caves; you needn't wait for dusk. The reeds and tallow throw a steadier light. Something is being turned inside out, here, for the first time: The pictures in the patterning brain are being projected, rendered. Our more recent ancestors will discover these stone screens, their images still expressing life and movement, and marvel at them, and not so long before the first moving images are projected.

WHAT WE CALL "media" were originally called "mass media," technologies allowing the replication of passive experience. As a novelist, I work in the oldest mass medium, the printed word. The book has been largely unchanged for centuries. Working in language expressed as a system of marks on a surface, I can induce extremely complex experiences, but only in an audience elaborately educated to experience this. This platform still possesses certain inherent advantages. I can, for instance, render interiority of character with an ease and specificity denied to a screenwriter. But my audience must be literate, must know what prose fiction is and understand how one accesses it. This requires a complexly cultural education, and a certain socioeconomic basis. Not everyone is afforded the luxury of such an education.

But I remember being taken to my first film, either a Disney animation or a Disney nature documentary (I can't recall which I saw first), and being overwhelmed by the steep yet almost instantaneous learning curve: In that hour, I learned to watch film. Was taught, in effect, by the film itself. I was years away from being able to read my first novel, and would need a lot of pedagogy to do that. But film itself taught me, in the dark, to view it. I remember it as a sort of violence done to me, as full of terror as it was of delight. But when I emerged from that theater, I knew how to watch film.

What had happened to me was historically the result of an immensely complex technological evolution, encompassing optics, mechanics, photography, audio recording, and much else. Whatever film it was that I first watched, other people around the world were also watching, having approximately the same experience in terms of sensory input. And that film no doubt survives today, in Disney's back catalog, as an experience that can still be accessed.

That survival, I think, is part of the key to understanding

where the digital may be taking us. In terms of most of our life so far, as a species, it's not a natural thing to see the dead, or hear their voices. I believe the significance of that is still far from being understood. We can actually see what life, at least in some very basic sense, was like, one hundred years ago. We can watch a silent movie, and not only see people who are long dead, but see people who were in their seventies and eighties in the 1920s, and who therefore bore the affect of their developing years—i.e., from before the Civil War, and earlier. It is as if in 1956 we had been able to watch silent film of, say, the Lincoln–Douglas debates, or the various revolutions of 1848. When the ramifications of this are really thought about, it becomes awesome in almost a religious sense.

Our ancestors, when they found their way to that first stone screen, were commencing a project so vast that it only now begins to become apparent: the unthinking construction of a species-wide, time-defying, effectively immortal prosthetic memory. Extensions of the human brain and nervous system, capable of surviving the death of the individual—perhaps even of surviving the death of the species. The start of building what would become civilization, cities, cinema. Vast stone calendars, megalithic machines remembering the need to plant on a given day, to sacrifice on another.

With the advent of the digital, which I would date from, approximately, World War II, the nature of this project begins to become more apparent, more overt; the texture of these more recent technologies, the grain of them, becomes progressively finer, progressively more divorced from Newtonian mechanics. In terms of scale, they are more akin to the workings of the brain itself.

All of us, creators or audience, have participated in the change so far. It's been something many of us haven't yet gotten a handle on. We are too much of it to see it. It may be that we never do get a handle on it, as the general rate of technological innovation shows no indication of slowing.

Much of history has been, often to an unrecognized degree, technologically driven. From the extinction of North America's mega-fauna to the current geopolitical significance of the Middle East, technology has driven change. (That's spear-hunting technology for the mega-fauna and the internal combustion engine for the Middle East, by the way.) Very seldom do nations legislate the emergence of new technologies.

The Internet, an unprecedented driver of change, was a complete accident, and that seems more often the way of things. The Internet is the result of the unlikely marriage of a DARPA project and the nascent industry of desktop computing. Had nations better understood the potential of the Internet, I suspect they might well have strangled it in its cradle. Emergent technology is, by its very nature, out of control, and leads to unpredictable outcomes.

As indeed does the emergent realm of the digital. I prefer to view this not as the advent of some new and extraordinary weirdness, but as part of the ongoing manifestation of some very ancient and extraordinary weirdness: our gradual spinning of a sort of extended prosthetic mass nervous-system, out of some urge that was present around the cooking fires of our earliest human ancestors.

We call film "film" today in much the same way we "dial" phones, the actual dials being long gone. The fact that we do still employ actual film, in the traditional sense, seems an artifact of platform transition and industrial economics. I tend to take arguments for the innate esthetic superiority of "film" with the same grain of salt I reserve for arguments for the innate esthetic superiority of vinyl. Whatever the current shortcomings of the digital image, I imagine there will be digital ways around them.

But I need to diverge here into another industry, one that's already and even more fully feeling the historical impact of the digital: music. Prior to the technology of audio recording, there was relatively little one could do to make serious money with music. Musicians could perform for money, and the printing press had given rise to an industry in sheet music, but great fame, and wealth, tended to be a matter of patronage. The medium of the commercial audio recording changed that, and created an industry predicated on an inherent technological monopoly of the means of production. Ordinary citizens could neither make nor manufacture audio recordings. That monopoly has now ended. Some futurists, looking at the individual musician's role in the realm of the digital, have suggested that we are in fact heading for a new version of the previous situation, one in which patronage (likely corporate, and nonprofit) will eventually become a musician's only potential ticket to relative fame and wealth. The window, then, in which one could become the Beatles, occupy that sort of market position, is seen to have been technologically determined. And technologically finite. The means of production, reproduction, and distribution of recorded music are today entirely digital, and thus are in the hands of whoever might desire them. We get them for free, often without asking for them, as inbuilt peripherals. I bring music up, here, and the impact the digital is having on it, mainly as an example of the unpredictable nature of technologically driven change. It may well be that the digital will eventually negate the underlying business model of popular musical stardom entirely. If this happens, it will be a change which absolutely no one intended, and few anticipated, and not the result of any one emergent technology, but of a complex interaction among several. You can see the difference if you compare the music industry's initial outcry against "home taping" with the situation today.

Whatever changes will come for film will be as unpredictable and as ongoing, but issues of intellectual property and piracy may ultimately be the least of them. The music industry's product is, for want of a better way to put it, a relatively simple, relatively traditional product. Audio recordings just aren't that technology-heavy. Though there's one aspect of the digital's impact on music that's absolutely central to film: sampling. Sampling music is possible because the end consumer of the product is now in possession of technologies equal or even superior to the technologies involved in producing that product. Human capital (that is, talent) aside, all the end-consumer-slash-creator lacks today, in comparison to a music-marketing conglomerate, is the funds required to promote product. The business of popular music, today, is now, in some peculiarly new way, entirely about promotion.

Film, I imagine, is in for a different sort of ride up the timeline, primarily owing to the technology-intensive nature of today's product. *Terminator III Unplugged* is a contradiction in terms. Hollywood is massively and multiply plugged, and is itself a driver of new technologies. The monopoly on the means of production (at least in terms of creation) can be preserved, in this environment, as the industry itself operates on something very near the cutting edge of emergent technology. For a while, at least.

In terms of the future, however, the history of recorded music suggests that any film made today is being launched up the timeline toward end-user technologies ultimately more intelligent, more capable, than the technologies employed in the creation of that film.

Which is to say that, no matter who you are, nor how pure your artistic intentions, nor what your budget was, your product, somewhere up the line, will eventually find itself at the mercy of people whose ordinary civilian computational capacity outstrips anything anyone has access to today.

Remember the debate around the ethics of colorizing films shot in black and white? Colorization, up the line, is a preference setting. Probably the default setting, as shipped from the factory.

I imagine that one of the things our great-grandchildren will find quaintest about us is how we had all these different, function-specific devices. Their fridges will remind them of appointments and the trunks of their cars will, if need be, keep the groceries from thawing. The environment itself will be smart, rather than various function-specific nodes scattered through it. Genuinely ubiquitous computing spreads like warm Vaseline. Genuinely evolved interfaces are transparent, so transparent as to be invisible.

This spreading, melting, flowing together of what once were distinct and separate media, that's where I imagine we're headed. Any linear narrative film, for instance, can serve as the armature for what we would think of as a virtual reality, but which Johnny X, eight-year-old end-point consumer, up the line, thinks of as how he looks at stuff. If he discovers, say, Steve McQueen in *The Great Escape*, he might idly pause to allow his avatar a freestyle Hong Kong kick-fest with the German guards in the prison camp. Just because he can. Because he's always been able to. He doesn't think about these things. He probably doesn't fully understand that that hasn't always been possible. He doesn't know that you weren't always able to explore the sets virtually, see them from any angle, or that you couldn't open doors and enter rooms that never actually appeared in the original film.

Or maybe, if his attention span wavers, he'll opt to experience the film as if shot from the POV of that baseball that McQueen keeps tossing.

Somewhere in the countless preferences in Johnny's system, there's one that puts high-rez, highly expressive dog heads on all of the characters. He doesn't know that this setting is based on a once-popular Edwardian folk motif of poker-playing dogs, but that's okay; he's not a history professor, and if he needed to know, the system would tell him. You get complete breed selection, too, with the dog-head setting, but that was all something he enjoyed more when he was still a little kid.

But later in the afternoon he's run across something called *The Hours*, and he's not much into it at all, but then he wonders how these women would look if he put the dog heads on them. And actually it's pretty good, then, with the dog heads on, so then he opts for the freestyle Hong Kong kick-fest. . . .

And what has happened, here, in this scenario, is that our ancient project, that began back at the fire, has come full circle. The patterns in the heads of the ancestors have come out, over many millennia, and have come to inhabit, atemporally, this nameless, single, nonphysical meta-artifact we've been constructing. So that they form an extension of Johnny's being, and he accesses them as such, and takes them utterly for granted, and treats them with no more respect than he would the products of his own idle surmise. But he's still a child, Johnny, and swims unknowing in this, his culture and the culture of his species. He'll be educated (likely via this same system he plays with now, in a more pedagogical mode—and likely, without his knowing, it's already doing that, in background as it were). It may be that he'll have to be taught to watch films, in the way that we watch them (or watched them, as I think DVDs are already changing that, not to mention changing the way you approach making them). He may need something akin to the sort of education that I needed in order to read novels—to appreciate, as it were, a marginalized but still powerfully viable media platform.

I can only trust that Johnny's entertainment system, and the culture that informs it, will be founded on solid curatorial principles. That there will be an ongoing archaeology of media product in place to ensure that someone or something is always there to categorically state, and if necessary to prove, that *The Maltese Falcon* was shot in black and white and originally starred Humphrey Bogart.

Because I see Johnny falling asleep now in his darkened bedroom, and atop the heirloom IKEA bureau, the one that belonged to his grandmother, which his mother has recently had restored, there is a freshly extruded resin action-figure, another instantaneous product of Johnny's entertainment system.

It is a woman, posed balletically, as if in flight on John Wu wires.

It is Meryl Streep, as she appears in *The Hours*.

She has the head of a Chihuahua.

This is one of many re-excavations of the material in "Dead Man Sings."

Note how blithely I skip, whistling, past any possibility whatever that the digital might do anything to (cough) the book, or to the means of the book's publication and distribution. Oh dear. I had my suspicions even then, but I seem to have been mainly bent, that day, on causing Hollywood directors the greatest possible anxiety.

Why on earth would anyone ever want to do that?

DISNEYLAND WITH THE DEATH PENALTY

WIRED

SEPTEMBER 1993

"IT'S LIKE AN ENTIRE COUNTRY run by Jeffrey Katzenberg," the producer had said, "under the motto 'Be happy or I'll kill you.'" We were sitting in an office a block from Rodeo Drive, on large black furniture leased with Japanese venture capital.

Now that I'm actually here, the Disneyland metaphor is proving impossible to shake. For that matter, Rodeo Drive comes frequently to mind, though the local equivalent feels more like thirty or forty Beverly Centers put end to end.

Was it Laurie Anderson who said that VR would never look real until they learned how to put some dirt in it? Singapore's airport, the Changi Airtropolis, seemed to possess no more resolution than some early VPL world. There was no dirt whatsoever; no muss, no furred fractal edge to things. Outside, the organic, florid as ever in the tropics, had been gardened into brilliant green, and all-too-perfect examples of itself. Only the clouds were feathered with chaos—weird columnar structures towering above the Strait of China.

The cab driver warned me about littering. He asked where I was from.

He asked if it was clean there. "Singapore very clean city."

One of those annoying Japanese-style mechanical bells cut in as he exceeded the speed limit, just to remind us both that he was doing it. There seemed to be golf courses on either side of the freeway. . . .

"You come for golf?"

"No."

"Business?"

"Pleasure."

He sucked his teeth. He had his doubts about that one.

Singapore is a relentlessly G-rated experience, micromanaged by a state that has the look and feel of a very large corporation. If IBM had ever bothered to actually possess a physical country, that country might have had a lot in common with Singapore. There's a certain white-shirted constraint, an absolute humorlessness in the way Singapore Ltd. operates; conformity here is the prime directive, and the fuzzier brands of creativity are in extremely short supply.

The physical past here has almost entirely vanished.

There is no slack in Singapore. Imagine an Asian version of Zurich operating as an offshore capsule at the foot of Malaysia; an affluent microcosm whose citizens inhabit something that feels like, well, Disneyland. Disneyland with the death penalty.

But Disneyland wasn't built atop an equally peculiar nineteenth-century theme park—something constructed to meet both the romantic longings and purely mercantile needs of the British Empire. Modern Singapore was: Bits of the Victorian construct, dressed in spanking-fresh paint, protrude at quaint angles from the white-flanked glitter of the neo-Gernsbackian metropolis. These few very deliberate fragments of historical texture serve as a reminder of just how deliciously odd an entrepôt Singapore once was—a product of Empire kinkier even than Hong Kong.

The sensation of trying to connect psychically with the old Singapore is rather painful, as though Disneyland's New Orleans Square had been erected on the site of the actual French Quarter, obliterating it in the process but leaving in its place a glassy simulacrum. The façades of the remaining Victorian shop-houses recall Covent Garden on some impossibly bright London day. I took several solitary, jet-lagged walks at dawn, when a city's ghosts tend to be most visible, but there was very little to be seen of previous realities: joss stick smoldering in an old brass holder on the white-painted column of a shop-house; a mirror positioned above the door of a supplier of electrical goods, set to snare and deflect the evil that travels in a straight line; a rusty trishaw, chained to a freshly painted iron railing. The physical past, here, has almost entirely vanished.

In 1811, when Temenggong, a local chief, arrived to resettle Singapura, the Lion City, with a hundred Malays, the jungle had long since reclaimed the ruins of a fourteenth-century city once warred over by Java, Siam, and the Chinese. A mere eight years later came Sir Stamford Raffles, stepping ashore amid a squirming tangle of kraits and river pirates, to declare the place a splendid spot on which to create, from the ground up, a British trading base. It was Raffles's singular vision to set out the various colonial jewels in Her Majesty's crown as distinct ethnic quarters: here Arab Street, here Tanjong Pagar (Chinese), here Serangoon Road (Indian). And Raffles's theme park boomed for a hundred and ten years—a free port, a Boy's Own fantasy out of Talbot Mundy, with every human spice of Asia set out on a neatly segmented tray of sturdy British china: "the Manchester of the East." A very hot ticket indeed.

When the Japanese came and took it all, with dismaying ease, the British dream-time ended; the postwar years brought rapid decay, and equally rapid aspirations for independence. In 1965, Mr. Lee Kuan Yew, a Cambridge-educated lawyer, became the country's first prime minister. Today's Singapore is far more precisely the result of Lee Kuan Yew's vision than the Manchester of the East ever was of Sir Stamford Raffles's. Lee Kuan Yew's People's Action Party has remained in power ever since; has made, some would say, quite drastically certain that it would do so. The emblem of the PAP is a cartoony lightning bolt striking within a circle; Reddy Kilowatt as the mascot of what is, in effect, a single-party capitalist technocracy.

FINANCE DATA A STATE SECRET

SINGAPORE—A government official, two private economists, and a newspaper editor will be tried jointly on June 21 for revealing an official Singaporean secret—its economic growth rate.

Business Times editor Patrick Daniel, Monetary Authority of Singapore official Shanmugaratnam Tharman, and two economists for regional brokerage Crosby Securities, Manu Bhaskaran and Raymond Foo Jong Chen, pleaded not guilty to violating Singapore's Official Secrets Act.

South China Morning Post, 4/29/93

Reddy Kilowatt's Singapore looks like an infinitely more livable version of convention-zone Atlanta, with every third building supplied with a festive party hat by the designer of Loew's Chinese Theater. Rococo pagodas perch atop slippery-flanked megastructures concealing enough cubic footage of atria to make up a couple of good-sized Lagrangian-5 colonies. Along Orchard Road, the Fifth Avenue of Southeast Asia, chockablock with multilevel shopping centers, a burgeoning middle class shops ceaselessly. Young, for the most part, and clad in computer-weathered cottons from the local Gap clone, they're a handsome populace; they look good in their shorts and Reeboks and Matsuda shades.

There is less in the way of alternative, let alone dissident, style in Singapore than in any city I have ever visited. I did once see two young Malayan men clad in basic, global, heavy metal black—jeans and T-shirts and waist-length hair. One's T-shirt was embroidered with the Rastafarian colors, causing me to think its owner must have balls the size of durian fruit, or else be flat-out suicidal, or possibly both. But they were it, really, for overt boho style. (I didn't see a single "bad" girl in Singapore. And I missed her.) A thorough scan of available tapes and CDs confirmed a pop diet of such profound middle-of-the-road blandness that one could easily imagine the stock had been vetted by Mormon missionaries.

"You wouldn't have any Shonen Knife, would you?"

"Sir, this is a music shop."

Although you don't need Mormons making sure your pop is squeaky clean when you have the Undesirable Propagation Unit (UPU), one of several bodies of official censors. (I can't say with any certainty that the UPU, specifically, censors Singapore's popular music, but I love the name.) These various entities attempt to ensure that red rags on the order of *Cosmopolitan* don't pollute the body politic. Bookstores in Singapore, consequently, are sad affairs, large busy places selling almost nothing I would ever want to buy—as though someone had managed to surgically neuter a W. H. Smith's. Surveying the science-fiction and fantasy sections of these stores, I was vaguely pleased to see that none of my own works seemed to be available. I don't know for a fact that the UPU had turned them back at the border, but if they had, I'd certainly be in good company.

The local papers, including one curiously denatured tabloid, *New Paper*, are essentially organs of the state, instruments of only the most desirable propagation. This ceaseless boosterism, in the service of order, health, prosperity, and the Singaporean way, quickly induces a species of low-key Orwellian dread. (The feeling that Big Brother is coming at you from behind a happy face does nothing to alleviate this.) It would be possible, certainly, to live in Singapore and remain largely in touch with what was happening elsewhere. Only certain tonalities would be muted, or tuned out entirely, if possible. . . .

Singaporean television is big on explaining Singaporeans to themselves. Model families, Chinese, Malay, or Indian, act out little playlets explicating the customs of each culture. The familial world implied in these shows is like *Leave It to Beaver* without The Beave, a sphere of idealized paternalism that can only remind Americans my age of America's most fulsome public sense of itself in the mid-1950s.

"Gosh, Dad, I'm really glad you took the time to explain the Feast of the Hungry Ghosts to us in such minutely comprehensive detail."

"Look, son, here comes your mother with a nutritious low-cholesterol treat of fat-free *lup cheong* and skimmed coconut milk."

And, in many ways, it really does seem like 1956 in Singapore; the war (or economic struggle, in this case) has apparently been won, an expanded middle class enjoys great prosperity, enormous public works have been successfully undertaken, even more ambitious projects are under way, and a deeply paternalistic government is prepared, at any cost, to hold at bay the triple threat of communism, pornography, and drugs.

The only problem being, of course, that it isn't 1956 in the rest of world. Though that, one comes to suspect, is something that Singapore would prefer to view as our problem. (But I begin to wonder, late at night and in the privacy of my hotel room—what might the future prove to be, if this view should turn out to be right?)

Because Singapore is one happening place, biz-wise. I mean, the future here is so bright. . . . What other country is preparing to clone itself, calving like some high-tech socioeconomic iceberg? Yes, here it is, the first modern city-state to fully take advantage of the concept of franchise operations Mini-Singapores! Many!

In the coastal city of Longkou, Shandong province, China (just opposite Korea), Singaporean entrepreneurs are preparing to kick off the first of these, erecting improved port facilities and a power plant, as well as hotels, residential buildings, and, yes, shopping centers. The project, to occupy 1.3 square kilometers, reminds me of "Mr. Lee's Greater Hong Kong" in Neal Stephenson's *Snow Crash*, a sovereign nation set up like so many fried-noodle franchises along the feeder routes of edge-city America. But Mr. Lee's Greater Singapore means very serious business, and the Chinese seem uniformly keen to get a franchise in their neighborhood, and pronto.

Ordinarily, confronted with a strange city, I'm inclined to look for the parts that have broken down and fallen apart, revealing the underlying social mechanisms; how the place is really wired beneath the lay of the land as presented by the Chamber of Commerce. This won't do in Singapore, because nothing is falling apart. Everything that's fallen apart has already been replaced with something new. (The word "infrastructure" takes on a new and claustrophobic resonance here; somehow it's all infrastructure.)

Failing to find any wrong side of the tracks, one can usually rely on a study of the nightlife and the mechanisms of commercial sex to provide some entree to the local subconscious. Singapore, as might be expected, proved not at all big on the more intense forms of nightlife. Zouk, arguably the city's hippest dance club (modeled, I was told, after the rave scenes in Ibiza), is a pleasant enough place. It reminded me, on the night I looked in, of a large Barcelona disco, though somehow minus the party. Anyone seeking more raunchy action must cross the Causeway to Johor, where Singaporean businessmen are said to sometimes go to indulge in a little of the down and dirty. (But where else in the world today is the adjoining sleazy border town Islamic?) One reads of clubs there having their licenses pulled for stocking private cubicles with hapless Filipinas, so I assumed that the Islamic Tijuana at the far end of the Causeway was in one of those symbiotic pressure-valve relationships with the island city-state, thereby serving a crucial psychic function that would very likely never be officially admitted.

Singapore, meanwhile, has dealt with its own sex industry in two ways: by turning its traditional red-light district into a themed attraction in its own right, and by moving its massage parlors into the Beverly Centers. Bugis Street, once famous for its transvestite prostitutes—the sort of place where one could have imagined meeting Noel Coward, ripped on opium, cocaine, and the local tailoring, just off in his rickshaw for a night of high buggery—had, when it proved difficult to suppress, a subway station dropped on top of it. "Don't worry," the government said, "we'll put it all back, just the way it was, as soon as we have the subway in." Needless to say, the restored Bugis Street has all the sexual potential of Frontierland, and the transvestites are represented primarily by a number of murals.

The heterosexual hand-job business has been treated rather

differently, and one can only assume that it was seen to possess some genuine degree of importance in the national Confucian scheme of things. Most shopping centers currently offer at least one "health center"—establishments one could easily take for slick mini-spas, but which in fact exist exclusively to relieve the paying customer of nagging erections. That one of these might be located between a Reebok outlet and a Rolex dealer continues to strike me as evidence of some deliberate social policy, though I can't quite imagine what it might be. But there is remarkably little, in contemporary Singapore, that is not the result of deliberate and no doubt carefully deliberated social policy.

Take dating. Concerned that a series of earlier campaigns to reduce the national birth rate had proven entirely too successful, Singapore has instituted a system of "mandatory mixers." I didn't find this particularly disturbing, under the circumstances, though I disliked the idea that refusal to participate is said to result in a "call" to one's employer. But there did seem to be a certain eugenic angle in effect, as mandatory dating for fast-track yuppies seemed to be handled by one government agency, while another dealt with the less educated. Though perhaps I misunderstood this, as Singaporeans seemed generally quite loath to discuss these more intimate policies of government with a curious foreign visitor who was more than twice as tall as the average human, and who sweated slowly but continuously, like an aged cheese.

Singapore is curiously, indeed gratifyingly devoid of certain aspects of creativity. I say gratifyingly because I soon found myself taking a rather desperate satisfaction in any evidence that such a very tightly run ship would lack innovative élan.

So, while I had to admit that the trains did indeed run on time, I was forced to take on some embarrassingly easy targets. Contemporary municipal sculpture is always fairly easy to make fun of, and this is abundantly true in Singapore. There was a pronounced tendency toward very large objects that resembled the sort of thing *Mad* magazine once drew to make us giggle at abstract art: ponderous lumps of bronze with equally ponderous holes through them. Though perhaps, like certain other apparently pointless features of the cityscape, these really served some arcane but highly specific geomantic function. Perhaps they were actually conduits for feng shui, and were only superficially intended to resemble Henry Moore as reconfigured by a team of Holiday Inn furniture designers.

But a more telling lack of creativity may have been evident in one of the city's two primal passions: shopping. Allowing for the usual variations in price range, the city's countless malls all sell essentially the same goods, with extraordinarily little attempt to vary their presentation. While this is generally true of malls elsewhere, and in fact is one of the reasons people everywhere flock to malls, a genuinely competitive retail culture will assure that the shopper periodically encounters either something new or something familiar in an unexpected context.

Singapore's other primal passion is eating, and it really is fairly difficult to find any food in Singapore about which to complain. About the closest you could come would be the observation that it's all very traditional fare of one kind or another, but that hardly seems fair. If there's one thing you can live without in Singapore, it's a Wolfgang Puck pizza. The food in Singapore, particularly the endless variety of street snacks in the hawker centers, is something to write home about. If you hit the right three stalls in a row, you might decide these places are a wonder of the modern world. And all of it quite safe to eat, thanks to the thorough, not to say nitpickingly Singaporean auspices of the local hygiene inspectors, and who could fault that? (Credit, please, where credit is due.)

But still. And after all. It's boring here. And somehow it's the same ennui that lies in wait in any theme park, but particularly in those that are somehow in a too aggressively spiffy state of repair. Everything painted so recently that it positively creaks with niceness, and even the odd rare police car sliding past starts to look like something out of a Chuck E. Cheese franchise. . . . And you come to suspect that the reason you see so few actual police is that people here all have, to quote William Burroughs, "the policeman inside."

And what will it be like when these folks, as they so manifestly intend to do, bring themselves online as the Intelligent Island, a single giant data-node whose computational architecture is more than a match for their Swiss-watch infrastructure? While there's no doubt that this is the current national project, one can't help but wonder how they plan to handle all that stuff without actually getting any on them? How will a society founded on parental (well, paternal, mainly) guidance cope with the wilds of X-rated cyberspace? Or would they simply find ways not to have to? What if, while information elsewhere might be said to want to be free, the average Singaporean might be said to want, mainly, not to rock the boat? And to do very nicely, thank you, by not doing so?

Are the faceless functionaries who keep Shonen Knife and *Cosmo* out of straying local hands going to allow access to the geography-smashing highways and byways of whatever the Internet is becoming? More important, will denial of such access, in the coming century, be considered even a remotely viable possibility by even the dumbest of policemen?

Hard to say. And therein, perhaps, lies Singapore's real importance. The overt goal of the national IT2000 initiative is a simple one: to sustain indefinitely, for a population of 2.8 million, annual increases in productivity of three to four percent.

IT, of course, is "information technology," and we can all be suitably impressed with Singapore's evident willingness to view such technology with the utmost seriousness. In terms of applied tech, they seem to have an awfully practical handle on what this stuff can do. The National Computer Board has designed an immigration system capable of checking foreign passports in thirty seconds, resident passports in fifteen. Singapore's streets are planted with sensor loops to register real-time traffic; the traffic lights are computer controlled, and the system adjusts itself constantly to optimize the situation, creating "green waves" whenever possible. A different sort of green wave will appear if a building's fire sensor calls for help: Emergency vehicles are automatically green-lighted through to the source of the alarm. The physical operation of the city's port, constant and quite unthinkably complex, is managed by another system. A "smart-card" system is planned to manage billings for cars entering the Restricted Zone. (The Restricted Zone is that part of central Singapore which costs you something to enter with a private vehicle. Though I suspect that if, say, Portland were to try this, the signs would announce the "Clean Air Zone," or something similar.)

They're good at this stuff. Really good. But now they propose to become something else as well: a coherent city of information, its architecture planned from the ground up. And they expect that whole highways of data will flow into and through their city. Yet they also seem to expect that this won't affect them. And that baffles us, and perhaps it baffles the Singaporeans that it does.

Myself, I'm inclined to think that if they prove to be right, what will really be proven will be something very sad; and not about Singapore, but about our species. They will have proven it possible to flourish through the active repression of free expression. They will have proven that information does not necessarily want to be free.

But perhaps I'm overly pessimistic here. I often am; it goes with the territory. (Though what could be more frightening, out here at the deep end of the twentieth century, than a genuinely optimistic science-fiction writer?) Perhaps Singapore's destiny will be to become nothing more than a smug, neo-Swiss enclave of order and prosperity, amid a sea of unthinkable . . . weirdness.

Dear God. What a fate.

Fully enough to send one lunging up from one's armchair in

the atrium lounge of the Meridien Singapore, calling for a taxi to the fractal-free corridors of the Airtropolis.

But I wasn't finished, quite. There'd be another night to brood about the Dutchman.

I haven't told you about the Dutchman yet. It looks like they're going to hang him.

MAN GETS DEATH FOR IMPORTING
1 KG OF CANNABIS

A Malayan man was yesterday sentenced to death by the High Court for importing no less than 1 kg of cannabis into Singapore more than two years ago.

Mat Repin Mamat, 39, was found guilty of the offense committed at the Woodlands checkpoint on October 9, 1991, after a five-day trial.

The hearing had two interpreters.

One interpreted English to Malay while the other interpreted Malay to Kelantanese to Mat Repin, who is from Kelantan.

The prosecution's case was that when Mat Repin arrived at the checkpoint and was asked whether he had any cigarettes to declare, his reply was no.

As he appeared nervous, the senior customs officer decided to check the scooter.

Questioned further if he was carrying any *barang* (thing), Mat Repin replied that he had a kilogram of *ganja* (cannabis) under the petrol tank.

> In his defense, he said that he did not know that the
> cannabis was hidden there.
>
> *The Straits Times,* 4/24/93

The day they sentenced Mat Repin, the Dutchman was also up on trial. Johannes Van Damme, an engineer, had been discovered in custody of a false-bottomed suitcase containing way *mucho barang*: 4.32 kilograms of heroin, checked through from Bangkok to Athens.

The prosecution made its case that Van Damme was a mule; that he'd agreed to transport the suitcase to Athens for a payment of US $20,000. Sniffed out by Changi smackhounds, the suitcase was pulled from the belt, and Van Damme from the transit lounge, where he may well have been watching Beaver's dad explain the Feast of the Hungry Ghosts on a wall-mounted Sony.

The defense told a different story, though it generally made about as much sense as Mat Repin's. Van Damme had gone to Bangkok to buy a wedding ring for his daughter, and had met a Nigerian who'd asked him, please, to take a suitcase through to Athens. "One would conclude," the lawyer for the defense had said, "that either he was a naïve person or one who can easily be made use of." Or, hell, both. I took this to be something akin to a plea for mercy.

Johannes Van Damme, in the newspaper picture, looks as thick as two bricks.

I can't tell you whether he's guilty or not, and I wouldn't want to have to, but I can definitely tell you that I have my doubts about whether Singapore should hang him, by the neck, until dead—even if he actually was involved in a scheme to shift several kilos of heroin from some back room in Bangkok to the junkies of the Plaka. It hasn't, after all, a whole hell of a lot to do with Singapore. But remember "Zero Tolerance"? These guys have it.

And, very next day, they announced Johannes Van Damme's death sentence. He still has at least one line of appeal, and he is still, the paper notes, "the first Caucasian" to find his ass in this particular sling.

"My ass," I said to the mirror, "is out of here." Put on a white shirt laundered so perfectly the cuffs could slit your wrists. Brushed my teeth, ran a last-minute check on the luggage, forgot to take the minibar's tinned Australian Singapore Sling home for my wife.

Made it to the lobby and checked out in record time. I'd booked a cab for four a.m., even though that gave me two hours at Changi. The driver was asleep, but he woke up fast, insanely voluble, the only person in Singapore who didn't speak much English.

He ran every red light between there and Changi, giggling. "Too early policeman . . ."

They were there at Changi, though, toting those big-ticket Austrian machine pistols that look like khaki plastic waterguns. And I must've been starting to lose it, because I saw a crumpled piece of paper on the spotless floor and started snapping pictures of it. They really didn't like that. They gave me a stern look when they came over to pick it up and carry it away.

So I avoided eye contact, straightened my tie, and assumed the position that would eventually get me on the Cathay Pacific's flight to Hong Kong.

In Hong Kong I'd seen huge matte black butterflies flapping around the customs hall, nobody paying them the least attention. I'd caught a glimpse of the Walled City of Kowloon, too. Maybe I could catch another, before the future comes to tear it down.

Traditionally the home of pork butchers, unlicensed denturists, and dealers in heroin, the Walled City still stands at the foot of a runway, awaiting demolition. Some kind of profound embarrassment to modern China, its clearance has long been made a condition of the looming change of hands.

Hive of dream. Those mismatched, uncalculated windows. How they seemed to absorb all the frantic activity of Kai Tak airport, sucking in energy like a black hole.

I was ready for something like that. . . .

I loosened my tie, clearing Singapore airspace.

I hear that things have changed for the better in Singapore, in the years since my visit, and I am glad. But the Singaporean government responded to this piece, at the time, by banning the import of Wired *magazine. So I would suppose that this could be said to have been the most controversial of the pieces collected here.*

I was subsequently accused, though not by the Singaporean

government, of a sort of perverse neocolonial Ludditism, but my complaint was never that Singapore was too cutting-edge contemporary, but that it was simply totalitarian. Though at least it was upfront about it, I would add today, from the perspective of a harsher era.

MR. BUK'S WINDOW

THE GLOBE AND MAIL

SEPTEMBER 2001

ALL THAT TERRIBLE WEEK I would think of the very small display window of E. Buk, a marvelously idiosyncratic antiques dealer in SoHo. E. Buk is never open. There is no shop directly behind the little window in a side street. A locked door, and, one assumes, stairs. A tarnished brass plaque suggests that you may be able to make an appointment. I never have, but when I happen on Mr. Buk's window (somehow I can never remember exactly where it is) I invariably stop, to gaze with amazement and admiration at the extraordinary things, never more than three, that he's dredged from time and collective memory. It's my favorite shop window in all of Manhattan, and not even London can equal it in its glorious peculiarity and Borgesian potency.

Gazing into E. Buk's window, for me, has been like gazing into the back reaches of some cave where Manhattan stores its dreams. There is no knowing what might appear there. Once, a stove-sized, florally ornate cast-iron fragment that might have been a leftover part of the Brooklyn Bridge. Once, a lovingly crafted plywood box containing exquisitely painted models of every ballistic missile in the arsenals of the U.S. and the U.S.S.R. at the time of its making. This last, redolent of both the Cold War and the Cuban Missile Crisis, had particularly held my attention. It was obviously a military learning aid, and I wondered what sort of lectures it had illustrated. It seemed, then, a relic from a dark and terrible time that I remembered increasingly as a dream, a very bad dream, of childhood.

But the image that kept coming to me, last week, was of the dust that must be settling on the ledge of E. Buk's window, more or less between Houston and Canal streets. And in that dust, surely, the stuff of the atomized dead. The stuff of pyre and blasted dreams.

So many.

The fall of their dust requiring everything to be back-read in its context, and each of Buk's chosen objects, whatever they may have been, that Tuesday: the dust a final collage element, the shadowbox made mortuary.

And that was a gift, I think, because it gave me something to start to hang my hurt on, a hurt I still scarcely understand or recognize; to adjust one of my own favorite and secret few square yards of Manhattan, of the world, to such an unthinkable fate.

They speak of certain areas in Manhattan now as "frozen zones," and surely we all have those in our hearts today, areas of disconnect, sheer defensive dissociation, awaiting the thaw. But how soon can one expect the thaw to come, in wartime?

I have no idea.

Last year I took each of my children for a first visit to New York. I'm grateful now for them both to have seen it, for the first time, before the meaning of the text was altered, in such a way, forever. I think of my son's delight in the aged eccentricities of a Village bagel restaurant, of my daughter's first breathless solo walk through SoHo. I feel as though they saw London as it was before the Blitz.

New York is a great city, and as such central to the history of civilization. Great cities can and invariably do bear such wounds. They suffer their vast agonies and they go on—carrying us, and civilization, and windows like Mr. Buk's, however fragile and peculiar, with them.

Written about two weeks after 9/11, this piece became part of my decision not to abandon a novel-in-progress. I had been having more trouble than usual, getting it started. A woman from New York wakes alone, in an absent friend's apartment, feeling something I could somehow neither describe nor name. My immediate assumption, the day after 9/11, was that the narrative, very deliberately not set in the future, couldn't continue. I felt I had no idea what a character from New York would feel, now, and to attempt to do so would be presumptuous. Meanwhile, I continued to talk and email with friends in New York. When The Globe and Mail asked for something about 9/11, I wrote this, and shortly thereafter was visited by a conviction that Cayce, the protagonist who so far had adamantly refused to reveal herself, had been gazing into Mr. Buk's window as the first plane arrived. And that that, and all that had happened subsequently, was the cold enormous inexplicable thing she wakes with in London.

In the book, eventually, the geography shifted. The window that catches her attention is on the wrong side of the street, and the street itself slightly to the north. As happens in prose perhaps as often as in dream.

SHINY BALLS OF MUD:

Hikaru Dorodango and Tokyu Hands

TATE MAGAZINE

SEPTEMBER/OCTOBER 2002

JAPAN, 1996: A woman's nineteen-year-old son hasn't been doing well in school. He goes into his room one evening and closes the door.

He only leaves his room when he's certain that she and his father are either absent or sleeping.

She stands silently before his door for hours, waiting for him to emerge.

He uses the kitchen when he's sure of his parents' absence, or the living room, watching television there or using the computer. He uses the bathroom, emptying whatever containers he keeps for this purpose.

She continues to slip his weekly allowance under the door, and assumes that he buys food and other supplies in all-night convenience stores, and from the ubiquitous vending machines.

He's twenty-five years old now.

She hasn't seen him for six years.

WHEN I FIRST VISITED the Shibuya branch of Tokyu Hands, I was looking for a particular kind of Japanese sink stopper: a perfectly plain black sphere of rubber, slightly larger than a golf ball and quite a bit heavier, on a length of heavy-duty stainless-steel ball chain.

An architect friend in Vancouver had shown one to me. He admired the design for its simplicity and functionality: It found the drain on its own, seating itself. I was going to Tokyo for the first time, so he drew a map to enable me to find Tokyu Hands, a store he said he couldn't quite describe, except that they had these stoppers and much more.

At first I misunderstood the name as Tokyo Hands, but once there, I learned that the store was a branch of the Tokyu department store chain. There's a faux-archaic Deco Asian spire atop the Shibuya store, with a trademark green hand, and I learned to navigate by that, finding my way from Shibuya Station.

As the Abercrombie & Fitch of my father's day was to the well-heeled sport fisherman or hunter of game, Tokyu Hands is to the amateur carpenter, or to people who take exceptionally good care of their shoes, or to those who construct working brass models of Victorian steam tractors.

Tokyu Hands assumes that the customer is very serious about something. If that happens to be shining a pair of shoes, and the customer is sufficiently serious about it, he or she may need the very best German sole-edge enamel available—for the museum-grade weekly restoration of the sides of the soles.

My own delight at this place, an entire department store radiating obsessive-compulsive desire, was immediate and intense. I had stumbled, I felt, upon some core aspect of Japanese culture, and everything I've learned since has only confirmed this.

America or England might someday produce a specialist department store combining DIY home repair with less practical crafts, but it wouldn't be Tokyu Hands.

LATER I WOULD DISCOVER Kyoichi Tsuzuki's photographs of the interiors of Japanese apartments: "cockpit living." Everything you own directly before you, constantly available to your gaze. The pleasures of a littered coziness in what to western eyes seem impossibly tiny spaces, like living in a Cornell box that's been through a mild earthquake (and likely it has). Deliberate yet gratuitous collections of things: a bachelor's apartment wall, stacked floor to ceiling with unopened plastic model-kits of military vehicles.

I suspected that these photographs brought me closer to grasping the mystery at the heart of Tokyu Hands, but still it remained just out of cultural reach.

AS MANY AS one million Japanese, the majority of them young males, have now retreated into their rooms, some for as little as six months, others for as long as ten years. Forty-one percent of them withdraw for from one to five years, yet relatively few of them display symptoms of agoraphobia, depression, or any other condition that would ordinarily be expected to account for such behavior.

A Japanese parent will not enter a child's room without permission.

VENDING MACHINES in Tokyo constitute a secret city of solitude.

Limiting oneself to purchases from vending machines, it's possible to spend entire days in Tokyo without having to make eye contact with another sentient being.

THE PARADOXICAL SOLITUDE and omnipotence of the *otaku*, the new century's ultimate enthusiast: the glory and terror inherent in the absolute narrowing of personal bandwidth.

HIKARU DORODANGO—shiny balls of mud.

Professor Fumio Kayo of the Kyoto University of Education first encountered these enigmatic, glistening spheres in a nursery school in Kyoto in 1999.

The *dorodango*, balls of mud compressed with the hands and painstakingly formed into perfect spheres, became the object of considerable media attention.

THE SILENT young men who must sometimes appear, blinking, in the unaccustomed glare of a Tokyo 7-Eleven at three in the morning, stocking up on white foam bowls of instant ramen, in their unlaundered, curiously outmoded clothing, are themselves engaged in the creation of *dorodango*, their chosen material: existence itself.

———

ABOUT THREE INCHES in diameter, the surface of a completed *dorodango* glistens with an illusion of depth not unlike that seen in traditional Japanese pottery glazes. A *dorodango* becomes its maker's greatest treasure.

Kayo has invented a scale for recording a *dorodango*'s luster, with the shiniest rating a 5. It took him two hundred attempts and analysis with an electron microscope to duplicate the children's results and produce an adequately lustrous *dorodango*.

The genesis of the making of *hikaru dorodango* remains an absolute mystery.

THE FLOORS of Tokyu Hands are haunted for me now with the mysterious, all-encompassing presence of the *hikaru dorodango*, an artifact of such utter simplicity and perfection that it seems it must be either the first object or the last, something that either instigated the Big Bang or awaits the final precipitous descent into universal silence. At the very end of things waits the *hikaru dorodango*, a perfect three-inch sphere of mud. At its heart: the unthinkable.

The secret of Tokyu Hands is that everything on offer there inclines, ultimately, to the status, if not the perfection, of *hikaru dorodango*. The brogues, shined lovingly enough, for long enough, with those meticulously imported shoe-care products, must ultimately become a universe unto themselves, a conceptual sphere of lustrous and infinite depth.

Just as a life, lived silently enough, in sufficient solitude, becomes a different sort of sphere, no less perfect.

Writing for the Tate's own magazine somehow provided an unusual sense of security, almost of privacy. With the result that I wish this were a novel, somehow.

AN INVITATION

PREFACE, LABYRINTHS, JORGE LUIS BORGES

2007

I FIRST READ Jorge Luis Borges's *Labyrinths* in an armchair upholstered with a smooth lettuce-green brocade, patterned with leaves that were themselves not unlike lettuce, though they were also rather like clouds, or perhaps rabbits. I regarded that chair as an environment in and of itself, having known it since earlier childhood. It was the only relatively safe place in a room I regarded as ominously formal and adult, a room dominated by large pieces of dark furniture belonging to my mother's family. One of these was an unnaturally tall desk, topped with a bookcase closed with two long and solid doors, reputed, though dimly, to have once belonged to the Revolutionary hero Francis Marion. Its lower drawers smelled terrifyingly and chemically of Time, and within them, furled, lay elaborately printed scrolls listing the county's dead in the Great War.

I now know that I believed, without quite wanting to admit it to myself, that that desk was haunted.

I initially discovered Borges in one of the more liberal-minded anthologies of science fiction, which had included his story "The Circular Ruins." That sufficiently intrigued me that I sought out *Labyrinths*, which I imagine would have been fairly difficult for me to find, though I no longer recall those difficulties.

I do, however, remember the sensation, both complex and eerily simple, induced by my first reading of "Tlön, Uqbar, Orbis Tertius," while seated in that green chair.

Had the concept of software been available to me, I imagine I would have felt as though I were installing something that exponentially increased what one day would be called bandwidth, though bandwidth of what, exactly, I remain unable to say. This sublime and cosmically comic fable of utterly pure information (i.e., the utterly fictive) gradually and relentlessly infiltrating and ultimately consuming the quotidian, opened something within me which has never yet closed.

Or without me, possibly, I hungrily and delightedly saw, as Borges's hallmark corridors of mirrors opened out around me in every direction. Decades later, now, I understand the word "meme," to the extent that I understand it at all, in terms of Tlön's viral message, its initial vector a few mysteriously extra pages in an otherwise seemingly ordinary volume of a less than stellar encyclopedia.

Works we all our lives recall reading for the first time are among the truest milestones, but *Labyrinths* was a profoundly singular one, for me, and I believe I knew that, then, in my early adolescence. It was demonstrated to me, that afternoon. Proven. For, by the time I had finished with "Tlön" (though one never finishes with "Tlön," nor indeed with any story by Borges) and had traversed "The Garden of Forking Paths" and wondered, literally bug-eyed, at "Pierre Menard, Author of the Quixote," I discovered that I had ceased to be afraid of any influence that might dwell within Francis Marion's towering desk.

Borges, this elegant and mysterious voice, whom I had instantly accepted as the most welcome of uncles, this inhabitant of a clearly mythical place called Buenos Aires, had somehow dissolved a great deal of childhood superstition. He had stretched basic paradigms as effortlessly, it seemed, as another gentleman might tip his hat and wink, and I had felt a certain crudeness, a certain foolishness, fall away.

I sat, changed, in the green chair, and regarded a different world, one whose underpinnings had been revealed to be at once infinitely more mysterious and far more interesting than I could previously have imagined.

When I left that room, I took Borges with me, and my life has been better for it, much better.

If you haven't yet made the gentleman's acquaintance, I can only urge you to do so. In all humility, I can serve no other function, here at the front of this now-venerable collection of his incomparable fictions, than to act, mercifully briefly, as a sort of butler. I am not a Borges scholar, nor indeed any sort of scholar, but I am honored (though indeed embarrassed, believing myself unworthy) to invite you in.

Please.

Many afternoons, decades, after my own introduction to Borges, I found myself in Barcelona, in late December, attending a festival celebrating his life and work. The events of the festival were staged in some vast repurposed fortress or castle, a structure I imagined had lain dusty and silent during the seeming centuries of Francisco Franco's ghastly rule, but which now, through the briskly confident resurgence of Catalan culture and vast amounts of European Union capital, hummed and gleamed like a vacuum tube within a thirteenth-century reliquary.

One afternoon, alone, I sought out a rumored display of manuscripts and other Borgesiana, in a hall on an upper floor. Finding this, I discovered that these objects were displayed beneath glass, but a glass treated in such a way as to approximate the effect of the onset of his glaucoma. They were visible, these relics, only narrowly, and in a way that imposed a painful and awkward dance of the head if they were to be studied closely. I remember the peculiarly childlike slope, from left to right, of a handwritten manuscript page, and the delicacy of a red-lacquered miniature Chinese birdcage, the gift of a poet friend.

I went out walking, then, after having been invited to meet later with Alberto Manguel in a bar on La Rambla, the only person I'd ever met to have actually known Borges. Manguel, when I had first met him, a decade before, had told me that he himself had met a man who had known Franz Kafka. And what had this person had to say about Kafka, I'd asked? That Kafka, Manguel had told me, had known everything there was to know about coffee. But now I could no longer remember if Manguel had had any information of that sort to impart about Borges, and I reminded myself to ask him, when we met.

Walking through Plaça Catalunya, I discovered a recent monument to some martyred Catalan figure in the civil war. It was grim, this monument, and terribly striking, a monolithic flight of granite stairs, tilted unnaturally, impossibly forward upon themselves, into the horizontal. A negation of what stairs are, and of flight, and of a life, aspiration. I stood beside it, shivering, trying to puzzle out the inscription. Failing to do so, I walked on, into La Rambla. And eventually met Manguel and his friends. And in the course of discussing his new place in the country, in France, forgot to bring up Borges.

A few days later, at home in Vancouver, I sat at my computer, watching live feed from a video camera positioned somewhere high on the side of a building, overlooking Plaça Catalunya. And on my screen was that terrible monument, the granite stairs, impossibly rotated, mute symbol of negation.

And beside it a man, wearing a brown coat, not unlike the one I had worn, standing. Attempting to puzzle out an inscription.

I was abetted, in that moment, by technologies Borges, our heresiarch uncle, with his doctrines of circular time, his invisible tigers, his paradoxes, his knife-fighters and mirrors and dawns, had no need of. And in that moment, as you will soon know if you are fortunate enough to ignore the awkwardness of our meeting here, and to enter that which awaits you, I knew myself, once again, to be within the labyrinth.

A ridiculously unearned honor, to be asked to do this. I'm still embarrassed.

HONK IF YOU LOVE BORGES *read a bumper sticker my editor once sent to me. I do.*

METROPHAGY:

The Art and Science of Digesting Great Cities

REVIEW OF LONDON: The Biography by
Peter Ackroyd, in The Whole Earth Catalog

SUMMER 2001

LITERARY FORMS ARE TOOLS, and genuinely new ones are few and far between.

I believe that Peter Ackroyd has invented a genuinely new one with *London: The Biography*, although I would hesitate to give him sole credit for the perfected form.

There has been a vast, multiauthored, peculiarly specific "London Project" rather cryptically under way for the past decade or so, in London, and Ackroyd of course has been central to that, with works like *Hawksmoor, The House of Doctor Dee,* and *Dan Leno and the Limehouse Golem.*

But these books arise from a substrate of more singular and less popularly visible literature: from Iain Sinclair's poetry (*Lud Heat, Suicide Bridge*), novels (*Downriver, Radon Daughters*) and superbly hallucinatory London-based nonfiction (*Lights Out for the Territory*), and from the obsessively detailed graphic-novel Ripperology of Alan Moore's *From Hell.* (Somewhere deep at the heart of all of this accumulated New Wave Londonology dwell the tygers and angels of William Blake, himself an artificer of what we would call graphic novels, were they to be produced today.) These are all works which attempt to re-Braille the Borgesian labyrinth that is London and its history, while regarding that retouching, that induction of the "return of the reforgotten," as a heroic and somehow utterly crucial project in and of itself.

I have been a keen visitant to this London Project almost from its start, as the enigma of this mysteriously "unknowable" city has been with me since I first went there in my early twenties. The paradox of this vast human settlement, this text laid out in the one human language I have immediate and effortless access to, yet which remains somehow resolutely "closed," has troubled me quietly and constantly, and I have returned there more repeatedly, and more determinedly, than to any other world city. Looking, always, for some key, some Rosetta stone.

I began to find that key, it seemed, in the Nineties, in Iain Sinclair's work, with its weird cod-occult forays into urban ley lines and secret centers of ancient and nameless power. Sinclair's almost autistic vision cut down into the very magma of the thing, providing handles for what had previously seemed unimaginable, unmanageable.

But Sinclair's faux Lovecraftian subtexts, like Moore's blood-drenched conspiracies in *From Hell*, finally lose traction in the way that all conspiracy theories do: The description of an underlying, literally occulted order is invariably less complex than the surface reality it supposedly informs. Conspiracy theories and the occult comfort us because they present models of the world that more easily make sense than the world itself, and, regardless of how dark or threatening, are inherently less frightening.

Ackroyd, in *London: The Biography*, quite resolutely resists that, while continuing to generate a subtle and spooky and to my mind entirely genuine sense of the way that, when we examine London, we draw close to thrones and dominions—and not of the most obvious sort.

Each of the book's seventy-nine chapters functions as a core-drill down into an extraordinary wealth of narrative, of voices, each chapter an exploratory essay assembled under a given rubric: women, riots, drunkenness, sacred sites, food, entertainments violent and otherwise, jails, music, plagues, murders, electricity, clocks, magic, lost rivers, the underground, the homeless, trees, the suburbs. . . .

It is this simple structure that I believe constitutes a new form, as I know of no other work of urban history that functions in quite this way, or that delivers what this book delivers. Luc Sante's *Low Life* comes to mind for New York, and Edward Seidensticker's *Low City, High City* for Tokyo, with Seidensticker perhaps coming closest to Ackroyd's accomplishment here: the presentation of a city's wholeness and fractal history in the most purely organic terms. To possess this book, or rather to allow oneself to be possessed by it, is the closest literature can bring us to owning London.

And the London Ackroyd gives us partakes entirely of that from which it springs, so that we possess an "echoic" city, in which certain locales are subject to an ongoing relooping of narrative, as when the homeless shelter today beneath the very church eaves which sheltered the homeless of centuries ago. It is a city in which, he suggests, subjective time flows differently, from one area to the next, and may have come to a near-complete halt in others. It is a city in which the eternal suffering of the poor may perpetually serve some mysterious and driving purpose in the life of the whole, some hidden dynamo of torture and sacrifice dating back to something stranger and less easily articulated than the hungry ghosts of *Hawksmoor*.

These are not observations that one could arrive at using any previous literary model of metropolitan history, but the result of a genuinely postmodern agenda, an entirely new and utterly compelling way to write about cities.

If you wish to possess the world's greatest city, read this book. If you would learn to expose the soul of a place, in the deepest and most thoroughly contemporary way, read it again.

I loved The Whole Earth Catalog, *in the Seventies, though it made me feel guilt. I loved it for the sense it gave that my generation might find new ways of sorting out the world's difficulties (which now seems terribly ironic). The guilt I felt was equally straightforward, and perhaps as fantastic: that I was not repairing an electricity-generating windmill with a Leatherman tool. It made me feel terribly lazy.*

When Bruce Sterling guest-edited an issue, many years later, and invited me to contribute, I decided that Peter Ackroyd's book constituted a tool. It was for me, certainly, in that it eventually contributed to helping me find a way to write fiction set in London, something I'd long wanted to do.

This piece sells Iain Sinclair short, by the way, as he's subsequently discovered and named, in works such as Hackney, That Rose Red Empire, *and* Ghost Milk, *the real monsters of the twenty-first-century city. He was never at fault; I was merely impatient.*

MODERN BOYS AND MOBILE GIRLS

THE OBSERVER
APRIL 2001

"WHY JAPAN?" I've been asked for the past twenty years or so. Meaning: Why has Japan been the setting for so much of my fiction? When I started writing about Japan, I'd answer by suggesting that Japan was about to become a very central, very important place in terms of the global economy. And it did. (Or rather, it already had, but most people hadn't noticed yet.) A little later, asked the same question, I'd say that it was Japan's turn to be the center of the world, the place to which all roads lead; Japan was where the money was and the deal was done. Today, with the glory years of the bubble long gone, I'm still asked the same question, in exactly the same quizzical tone: "Why Japan?"

Because Japan is the global imagination's default setting for the future.

The Japanese seem to the rest of us to live several measurable clicks down the timeline. The Japanese are the ultimate Early Adaptors, and the sort of fiction I write behooves me to pay serious heed to that. If you believe, as I do, that all cultural change is essentially technologically driven, you pay attention to the Japanese. They've been doing it for more than a century now, and they really do have a head start on the rest of us, if only in terms of what we used to call "future shock" (but which is now simply the one constant in all our lives).

Consider the Mobile Girl, that ubiquitous feature of contemporary Tokyo street life: a schoolgirl busily, constantly messaging on her mobile phone (which she never uses for voice communication if she can avoid it). The Mobile Girl can convert pad strokes to *kanji* faster than should be humanly possible, and rates her standing in her cellular community according to the amount of numbers in her phone's memory. What is it that the Mobile Girls are so busily conveying to one another? Probably not much at all: the equivalent of a schoolgirl's note, passed behind the teacher's back. Content is not the issue here, but rather the speed, the weird unconscious surety, with which the schoolgirls of Tokyo took up a secondary feature (text messaging) of a new version of the cellular telephone, and generated, almost overnight, a microculture.

A little over a hundred years ago, the equivalent personal, portable techno-marvel in Tokyo would have been a mechanical watch. The printmakers of the Meiji period made a very large watch the satiric symbol of the westernized dandy, and for the Japanese, clock-time was an entirely new continuum, a new reality.

The techno-cultural suppleness that gives us Mobile Girls today is the result of a traumatic and ongoing temporal dislocation that began when the Japanese, emerging in the 1860s from a very long period of deep cultural isolation, sent a posse of bright young noblemen off to England. These young men returned bearing word of an alien technological culture they must have found as marvelous, as disconcerting, as we might find the products of reverse-engineered Roswell space junk. These Modern Boys, as the techno-cult they spawned came popularly to be known, somehow induced the nation of Japan to swallow whole the entirety of the Industrial Revolution. The resulting spasms were violent, painful, and probably inconceivably disorienting. The Japanese bought the entire train set: clock-time, steam railroads, electric telegraphy, western medical advances. Set it all up and yanked the lever to full on. Went mad. Hallucinated. Babbled wildly. Ran in circles. Were destroyed. Were reborn.

Were reborn, in fact, as the first industrialized nation in Asia. Which got them, not too many decades later, into empire-building expansionist mode, which eventually got them two of their larger cities vaporized, blown away by an enemy wielding a technology that might as well have come from a distant galaxy.

And then that enemy, their conquerors, the Americans, turned up in person, smilingly intent on an astonishingly ambitious program of cultural re-engineering. The Americans, bent on restructuring the national psyche from the roots up, inadvertently plunged the Japanese several clicks further along the timeline. And then left, their grand project hanging fire, and went off to fight Communism instead.

The result of this stupendous triple-whammy (catastrophic industrialization, the war, the American Occupation) is the Japan that delights, disturbs, and fascinates us today: A mirror world, an alien planet we can actually do business with, a future.

But had this happened to any other Asian country, I doubt the result would have been the same. Japanese culture is "coded," in some wonderfully peculiar way that finds its nearest equivalent, I think, in English culture. And that is why the Japanese are subject to various kinds of Anglophilia, and vice versa. It accounts for the totemic significance, to the Japanese, of Burberry plaid, and for the number of Paul Smith outlets in Japan, and for much else besides. Both nations display a sort of fractal coherence of sign and symbol, all the way down into the weave of history. And Tokyo is very nearly, in its own way, as "echoic" (to borrow Peter Ackroyd's term) a city as London.

I've always felt that London is somehow the best place from which to observe Tokyo, perhaps because the British appreciation of things Japanese is the most entertaining. There is a certain tradition of "Orientalia," of the faux Oriental that has been present here for a long time, and truly, there is something in the quality of a good translation that can never be captured in the original.

London, being London and whatever else, eminently assured of its ability to do whatever it is that London's always done, can reflect Japan, distort it, enjoy it, in ways that Vancouver, where I live, never can. In Vancouver, we cater blandly to the Japanese, both to the tour-bus people with the ever-present cameras and to a delightful but utterly silent class of Japanese slackers. These latter seem to jump ship simply to be here, and can be seen daily about the city, in ones and twos, much as, I suspect, you or I might seem to the residents of Puerto Vallarta. "There they are again. I wonder what they might be thinking?"

But we don't reflect them back. We don't have any equivalent of the robot sushi bar in Harvey Nichols, which is as perfectly

"Japanese" a thing as I've seen anywhere, and which probably wouldn't look nearly as cool if it had been built in Tokyo or Osaka.

We don't have branches of Muji interspersed between our Starbucks (although I wish we did, because I'm running out of their excellent toothpaste). Muji is the perfect example of the sort of thing I'm thinking of, because it calls up a wonderful Japan that doesn't really exist. A Japan of the mind, where even toenail clippers and plastic coat hangers possess a Zen purity: functional, minimal, reasonably priced. I would very much like to visit the Japan that Muji evokes. I would vacation there and attain a new serenity, smooth and translucent, in perfect counterpoint to natural fabrics and unbleached cardboard. My toiletries would pretend to be nothing more than what they are, and neither would I. (If Mujiland exists anywhere, it's probably not in Japan. If anywhere, it may actually be here, in London.)

Because we don't reflect them back, in Vancouver, they don't market to us in the same way they market to you.

The trendy watch chains of London are the only places in the world, aside from Japan, where one can purchase the almost-very-latest Japan-only product from Casio and Seiko.

Because Japanese manufacturers know that you see them, in London. They know that you get it. They know that you are a market.

I like to watch the Japanese in Portobello Market. Some are there for the crowd, sightseeing, but others are there on specific, narrow-bandwidth, obsessional missions, hunting British military watches or Victorian corkscrews or Dinky Toys or Bakelite napkin rings. The dealers' eyes still brighten at the sight of a tight shoal of Japanese, significantly sans cameras, sweeping determinedly in with a translator in tow. A legacy from the affluent days of the bubble, perhaps, but still the Japanese are likely to buy, should they spot that one particular object of *otaku* desire. Not an impulse buy, but the snapping of a trap set long ago, with great deliberation.

The *otaku*, the passionate obsessive, the information age's embodiment of the connoisseur, more concerned with the accumulation of data than of objects, seems a natural crossover figure in today's interface of British and Japanese cultures. I see it in the eyes of the Portobello dealers, and in the eyes of the Japanese collectors: a perfectly calm train-spotter frenzy, murderous and sublime. Understanding *otaku*-hood, I think, is one of the keys to understanding the culture of the Web. There is something profoundly postnational about it, extra-geographic. We are all curators, in the postmodern world, whether we want to be or not.

The Japanese are great appreciators of what they call "secret brands," and in this too they share something with the British. There is a similar fascination with detail, with cataloging, with distinguishing one thing from another. Both cultures are singularly adroit at reconceptualizing foreign product, at absorbing it and making it their own.

Why Japan, then? Because they live in the future, but neither yours nor mine, and somehow make it seem either interesting or comical or really interestingly dreadful. Because they are capable of naming an après-sport drink Your Water. Because they build museum-grade reproductions of the MA-1 flight jacket that require prospective owners to be on waiting lists for several years before one even has a chance of possibly, one day, owning the jacket. Because they can say to you, with absolute seriousness, believing that it means something, "I like your lifestyle!"

Because they are Japanese, and you are British, and I am American (or possibly Canadian, by this point).

And I like both your lifestyles.

Enjoy one another!

This is still the closest I've gotten to explaining why Japan fascinates me.

I actually feel I shouldn't have to. It's like being asked to explain why London fascinates me. Who asks a question like that?

Were Japanese girls the first power texters? They were the first I encountered.

I saw my first fax machine in Tokyo. Katsuhiro Otomo had several in his house, when he was making Akira. Joi Ito and his friends, in Tokyo, were the first people I saw using those tiny little newfangled cellphones to coordinate smoothly frenetic urban evenings. A fashionably dressed man in Floral Street, outside Paul Smith, was the first headset-equipped cellphone user I ever mistook for a talkative madman.

Thus is the future distributed.

MY OBSESSION

WIRED

JANUARY 1999

WHEN I WAS A YOUNG MAN, traversing the Seventies in whatever post-hippie, preslacker mode I could manage, I made a substantial part of my living, such as it was, in a myriad of minuscule supply-and-demand gaps that have now largely closed. I was what antique dealers call a "picker," a semi-savvy haunter of Salvation Army thrift shops, from which I would extract objects of obscure desire that I knew were upmarketable to specialist dealers, who sold in turn to collectors. To this day I am often unable to resist a professionally quick, carefully dispassionate scan over the contents of any thrift shop, though I almost never buy anything there. Mainly because the cut-rate treasures, the "scores" of legend, are long gone. The market has been rationalized. We have become a nation, a world, of pickers.

There are several reasons for this. One has to do with boomer demographics and the cult of nostalgia. There are now more fiftysomethings than there are primo childhood artifacts of a similar vintage. Most of our toys, unlike the wood and pot-metal of yore, were extrusion-molded ephemera, fragile styrene simulacra, highly unlikely to survive the random insults of time. A great deal of the boomer's remembered world has been melted down, or crushed into unreadable fragments in forgotten strata of landfill. What remains, particularly if it's "mint in box," becomes increasingly rarefied.

Another reason, and this one is more mysterious, has to do with an ongoing democratization of connoisseurship, in which curatorial privilege is available at every level of society. Whether one collects Warhol prints or Beanie Babies becomes, well, a matter of taste.

The idea of the Collectible is everywhere today, and sometimes strikes me as some desperate instinctive reconfiguring of the postindustrial flow, some basic mammalian response to the bewildering flood of sheer stuff we produce.

But the main driving force in the tidying of the world's attic, the drying up of random, "innocent" sources of rarities, is information technology. We are mapping literally everything, from the human genome to Jaeger two-register chronographs, and our search engines grind increasingly fine.

"Surely you haven't been bitten by the eBay bug," said my publishing friend Patrick. We were in the lobby of a particularly bland hotel somewhere within the confines of a New England technology park, and I was in fact feeling twinges of withdrawal.

eBay, which bills itself as Your Personal Trading Community™, is a site that hosts well over 800,000 online auctions per day, in 1,086 categories. eBay gets around 140 million hits per week, and, for the previous few months, a certain number of those hits had been from me.

And, in the process of adding to eBay's gargantuan hit-pile, several days before, I had gotten myself in trouble. In Uruguay.

How this happened: I'm home in Vancouver, midway through that first cup of morning coffee, in front of the computer, ready to work straight from the dreamstate.

I am deep into eBay, half awake, staring at a scan of this huge-ass Zenith diver's watch. And I am, mind you, a practicing ectomorph. I have wrists like pipe stems. I am not going to get too much wear out of a watch that's actually wider than my wrist.

But a little knowledge is a dangerous thing, and I know, having already become a habitué of eBay's Clocks, Timepieces: Wristwatches, that the movement in this particular Zenith is the very one Rolex installs in the big-ticket Daytona. Making this both a precision timepiece and possibly an undervalued one— the identical thing having sold on eBay, the week before, albeit in better cosmetic condition, for around two grand.

"I didn't even know you had Web access," Patrick said. "You mean you've overcome your infamous resistance to using the Net, but only in order to service an eBay addiction?"

Well, yes. Sort of. Not exactly.

eBay is simply the only thing I've found on the Web that keeps me coming back. It is, for me anyway, the first "real" virtual place.

In Patrick's hotel room, we used his laptop to get onto eBay, where I discovered that, yes, I was still high bidder for the damned Zenith: $500 American. This bid, you see, was the result of Fiddling Around. I'd sat there in my office, not quite awake yet, and had poked around with modest but increasingly higher bids, assuming that the seller's hidden "reserve," the lowest bid he'd accept, would be quite high. But no, at $500 I hit it, and suddenly I was listed there as high bidder. This had happened before, and I had always been outbid later. So I didn't worry.

But I didn't really want to have to buy this very large watch. Which was in Uruguay. And now I was still high bidder, and the auction would be run off before I got back to Vancouver. I thought about having to resell the Zenith.

When I did get back, though, I discovered, to mixed emotions, that I'd been "sniped." Someone, or rather their automated bidding software, had swooped in, in the last few seconds, and scooped the Zenith for only the least allowable increment over my bid.

How did I get into this, anyway?

I went happily along for years, smugly avoiding anything that involved a modem. E-mail address? Sorry. Don't have one.

And then I got a website. Had one foisted upon me, actually, and quite brilliantly, by Christopher Halcrow, who created "William Gibson's Yardshow," an "official" home page. So I kept having to go into my kids' bedrooms and beg for Web access to look at it, which bugged them.

Then Chris, who knows a bargain when he sees one, happened to buy this Performa 5200CD from someone who was leaving town. He passed the Performa on to me for what he'd paid for it, and suddenly I had this video-ready machine I could look at my site on, and the video-ready part brought cable into the office, so I got a cable modem, because it was faster, and I already had a hole drilled in the wall, and then I discovered that, damn, I had an e-mail address. It was part of the deal. So e-mail, over the course of about fifteen minutes, replaced the faxes I'd been using to keep in touch with certain people.

In the way of things, very shortly, I no longer had a website, Chris having found it necessary to get a life. But there was the rest of the Web, waiting to be explored. And I did, and promptly got bored. It was fun, at first, but then gradually I found that there wasn't really anywhere in particular I wanted to go. I went a lot of places, but I seldom went back.

Then I found eBay. And I wanted to go back. Because eBay is, basically, just a whole bunch of stuff. Stuff you can look at and wonder if you want—or let yourself want and then bid on.

Mechanical watches are so brilliantly unnecessary.

Any Swatch or Casio keeps better time, and high-end contemporary Swiss watches are priced like small cars. But mechanical watches partake of what my friend John Clute calls the Tamagotchi Gesture. They're pointless in a peculiarly needful way; they're comforting precisely because they require tending.

And vintage mechanical watches are among the very finest fossils of the predigital age. Each one is a miniature world unto itself, a tiny functioning mechanism, a congeries of minute and mysterious moving parts. Moving parts! And consequently these watches are, in a sense, alive. They have heartbeats. They seem to respond, Tamagotchi-like, to "love," in the form, usually, of the expensive ministrations of specialist technicians. Like ancient steam tractors or Vincent motorcycles, they can be painstakingly restored from virtually any stage of ruin.

And, as with the rest of the contents of the world's attic, most of the really good ones are already in someone's collection.

But the best of what's still available, below the spookily expensive level of a Sotheby's watch auction, can still be had for a few thousand dollars at most. At the time of this writing, the most desirable vintage Rolex on one New York dealer's website, a stainless-steel "bubble back" automatic, is priced at $3,800, a fraction of the cost of many contemporary watches by the same maker. (And it's so much cooler, possesses so much more *virtu*, than one of those gold-and-diamond Pimpomatic numbers!)

My father bought a stainless-steel Rolex Oyster with a stainless band at a duty-free in Bermuda in the early Fifties.

After his death, not very long after, my mother put it away in a bank vault, from whence I wheedled it when I was eighteen or so. I had a Rolex dealer in Tucson replace its white dial with a black one, so that it would be more like the one James Bond wore in Fleming's novels. I loved it, and, one very sad night a few years later, I sold it for very little to a classmate of mine, in order to pay for a hotel room in which to enjoy, if that's the word, a final bitter tryst with my high school sweetheart. It was one of those dumb-ass, basically self-destructive gestures, and I actually don't regret it. I needed that hotel room. But I've always missed that watch, that Rolex Oyster Precision, and have always had it in the back of my mind to replace it one day with another of similar vintage. I had never done anything about it, though, and made do quite happily with quartz. My last quartz watch was a French faux-military job I bought at the airport in Cannes, on my way home from the film festival. Cost about a hundred dollars. Perfectly adequate for everything—everything except the Tamagotchi Gesture.

Last year, for some reason, I was struck by an ad, one that ran repeatedly in the British men's fashion magazines, for the Oris "Big Crown Commander." It was just a very good-looking watch, I thought, and it was Swiss, and mechanical, and not terribly expensive as such things go. Driven in part by my then brand-new Web access, I used a search engine to determine that Oris had no Canadian distributor. This made the watch seem even cooler, so I went on, via the Web, to locate a Seattle retailer who carried what a sarcastic friend had taken to calling the Big Dick Commando. (The crown, the bit you twist to set it, see, is rather more than usually prominent, so that you can do it without removing your whacking great RAF pilot's gloves.)

And I was and am quite happy with it.

Except that, though I didn't know it at the time, my search for the Big Crown Commander had inadvertently exposed me to the eBay bug.

I got a little compulsive, eventually.

I found myself coming down to my basement office every morning and going straight to that one particular bookmark. New auctions are posted daily on eBay, so there was always something new to look at.

The first watch I bought was a Croton Aquamedico, a rarish— or obscure, depending on how you look at it—Swiss manual-wind from the late Forties or early Fifties, black dial with a white medical chapter ring. (Getting the terminology down was a big part of the kick, for me; a medical chapter ring is an outer, 60-second set of graduations that facilitate taking a patient's pulse.) It had been listed by a seller who didn't seem to be particularly into watches; the language of the listing was casual, nonspecialist, and not much mention was made of the watch's condition. E-mail to the seller elicited the opinion that the watch looked as though "it hadn't been worn very often," which I liked. The scan was intriguingly low-rez, but I really liked the design of the numerals. And I really liked its name, Aquamedico, which for some reason evoked for me the back pages, circa 1956, of *Field & Stream* and *True*.

Tentatively (but compulsively) I placed a low bid and waited to see if the Aquamedico attracted much attention from the eBay watch buffs. It didn't.

In the meantime, I determined that Croton was a long-established Swiss maker whose watches had been a lot more prominent in the United States in the Forties and Fifties. Full-page ads in wartime *Fortune*.

I decided to go for it. To try and buy this thing. To import a unique object, physically, out of cyberspace. Well, out of Pennsylvania, actually, but I did experience this peculiar yearning to turn the not-so-clear scan on my screen into a physical object on my desk. And for all I knew, it might be the only Croton Aquamedico left, anywhere. (And in fact I've only ever seen one other Aquamedico since on eBay, and it was gold-filled with a white dial, neither of which I liked as much.)

On the night of the auction, after having carefully considered bidding strategy (and this with no prior experience of bidding in any kind of auction), I placed a bid for considerably less than the two-hundred-dollar limit I'd set for myself.

That put me in high-bidder position. And then I sat there.

What if, it occurred to me, someone noticed my Croton in the auction's last few minutes and decided to grab it? eBay's system of proxy bidding encourages buyers to offer the most they're willing to pay for an item—their "maximum" bid. My maximum bid was a hundred and forty dollars. But on eBay you don't necessarily end up having to pay your maximum bid. In an auction house, if you raised your hand to bid two hundred dollars on a watch, you'd be on the hook for that amount. But on eBay, each auction has a set "bid increment"—with some as little as five cents. With a two-dollar set bid increment, a rival could bid two hundred dollars on my watch, beat me out, and end up having to pay only a hundred forty-two dollars, or two dollars over my maximum.

I started to get nervous. (And this, mind you, was before I even knew about sniping software and autobid bots.) What if someone else got this watch, this watch I'd never seen but which I now, somehow, was emotionally invested in winning? I began to have some sense of the power of the psychology of auctions, something I hadn't really experienced before.

I'm not a gambler. I've never put money on a horse, bought a lottery ticket, or bet on a hand of cards. Just doesn't do it for me. I've engaged in compulsive risk-taking behavior, certainly, but not the kind involving games of chance. But here, I recognized, I was starting to experience a buzz that I suspected was very much like a gambling buzz.

And what if, I asked myself, the Croton was really not all that desirable an object, a lemon, something a serious watch-nerd would find laughable?

What if the seller simply cashed my money order and did a runner? But I'd already checked his profile in the Feedback Forum, and there were lots of people on record there as saying he was honest, prompt, goods as described, and pleasant to deal with. (All of which turned out to be true.)

Meanwhile, with less than an hour to go before the auction closed, I was robotically punching the Netscape Reload button like a bandit-cranking Vegas granny, in case somebody outbid me. I knew how long it would take me to counterbid (not long), but I didn't know how quickly I could expect the server to process my bid.

Into the final countdown, nobody else showing up, when one more click on the Reload button produced . . . a new high bidder! Galvanized, I scrambled frantically through the bid process, and hit Bid. Real heart-in-mouth stuff, this. And, I must say, really fun.

Reload. And I was back, reinstated.

The auction closed.

The Aquamedico was mine.

I examined the address of the buyer who'd tried to outbid me at the last minute. An "hk" suggested that he was out of Hong Kong, which I already knew to be a hotbed of serious vintage-watch action. (The day before, I had found a wonderfully bizarre site in Taiwan, a sort of micro wrecker's yard, exclusively devoted to selling parts of Rolex watches: cases, dials, hands, etc.) I loved it that this Hong Kong bidder had popped in at the last minute, hoping to scoop what he, with his no doubt very considerable watch-savvy, knew to be an extremely desirable piece. But I had been there, ready, and I had prevailed.

I e-mailed the seller, sending my physical address and asking for his.

In the morning, I went out to buy a postal money order, the standard medium of exchange on eBay.

When the Aquamedico arrived, however, I was dismayed to find that it was peculiarly small, probably a "boy's" watch. I went back to its page on eBay and noted that, yes, it was indeed described as being a 30 mm watch. But the scan was larger than the watch itself, and I had assumed that 30 mm was standard (36 mm is actually closer to the contemporary men's standard). And while the steel case was very nearly mint, even better than the description, the crystal was in such rough shape that it was impossible to get a clear idea of the condition of the dial and hands. It had arrived from cyberspace, but it didn't really look like the scan. It looked as though it had been sitting in a sock drawer, somewhere in Pennsylvania, for fortysome years. Which it probably had.

But the seller's performance had been excellent, so I added my own note of positive feedback to his profile, and he gave me one in turn.

I took the Aquamedico to Otto Friedl, elite specialist in the care of vintage Swiss Tamagotchis, down in the lower lobby of the Hotel Vancouver, and asked to have it cleaned, lubricated, and the crystal replaced. When I went back for it, I discovered that it was a beautiful object indeed, the black dial immaculate, *virtu* intact.

But it wasn't "the watch."

I told myself that there wasn't any "the watch," and that I had simply found my own way, after avoiding it for years, of compulsively wasting time on the Net.

But I kept doing it. Opening that same bookmark and clicking down through pages and pages of watches. Learning to read a restricted code. And there was everything, really: Swatches (which are collected like Barbies), the same battered Gruens you would see gathering dust in a Kansas City pawnshop, every sort and vintage of Rolex, wartime Omegas with the British broad arrow stamped into the case back, German Sinn chronographs that you aren't really supposed to be able to buy here, Spiro Agnew campaign watches . . .

And bidding. I'd bid a few times per week and was usually content to let myself be outbid. But I did buy another watch, from London, an oddly named Tweka with a two-tone copper dial. It went for around a hundred fifty dollars and had been listed as "NOS," which means new old stock, something that supposedly has sat in the back of a jeweler's drawer since 1952. Very nice, after a trip to Otto, but still not the watch . . .

eBay is a cross between a swap meet in cyberspace and a country auction with computer-driven proxy bidding. The auctioneer is one of eBay's servers.

Buyers don't pay anything to eBay; they just pay sellers for the items they buy. Sellers, however, pay a fee on each item they list, and another fee if it sells. You can set this up so that your eBay seller's account comes off your credit card. I doubt if anyone's seller account amounts to much in a given month, but eBay moves a lot of items.

There's a sense of taking part in an evolving system, here. I suspect that eBay is evolving in much the way the Net did.

I started visiting eBay just as user IDs were coming in. You can opt to do business on eBay under a handle. I think that this was introduced in order to foil spam-miners, who were sending bots into eBay to scoop up e-mail addresses. And I actually did get spam, my very first, after my initial foray into eBay. But then I got a user ID and the spam stopped.

Looking over the Announcement Board recently, I saw that eBay now requires credit card information before allowing users into such categories as firearms and X-rated adult material: an age-checking strategy.

One thing I can imagine changing on eBay is the current requirement that sellers who want to display scans of their items find an off-site page on which to host their HTML. eBay links to tutorials on how to do this, but it's just enough of a learning curve to discourage some people. Myself included. If it were possible to send a scan directly to eBay, I think selling would take a major step toward becoming a ubiquitous activity.

I find clutter, in my personal environment, oppressive. But crazed environments of dead tech and poignant rubbish turn up in my fiction on a regular basis, where they are usually presented as being at once comforting, evocative, and somehow magical. The future as flea market. I really do tend to see the future that way, though not exclusively.

My first impulse, when presented with any spanking-new piece of computer hardware, is to imagine how it will look in ten years' time, gathering dust under a card table in a thrift shop. And it probably will.

The pleasure afforded by browsing eBay is the pleasure afforded by any flea market or garage sale. Something ruminative, but with an underlying acuity, as though some old hunter-gatherer module were activated. It's a lot like beachcombing.

Where eBay departs the traditional pleasure of a flea market, though, is in its sheer scale and its searchability. If you can think of a thing, you can search it on eBay. And, very probably, you can find it.

If randomness is what you're after, though, there are ways to surf eBay, rather than search it. Modes of sheer drift. Every item offers you a chance to peruse Seller's Other Auctions, which can take you off into categories of merchandise you wouldn't have thought of. A search for Hopi silver, for instance, brought up other kinds of Native American artifacts, much older ones, so that a series of clicks through stone adzes and Clovis points led to an obscure monograph on mound-excavation in Florida in the 1930s.

But it was the watches that kept me coming back.

And I started to get sniped.

I'd find a watch I wanted, work my way up to high-bidder position, check my position regularly (eBay regularly informs you of your bidding status, and outbid notices arrive promptly, but it's still fun to check), and find, as the auction ran off, that

I'd been zapped, in the last five minutes of bidding, by someone offering just one increment more than I had bid. I began to smell a rat.

The nature of the rat became apparent when I started checking out "Dutch" (multiple buyer) auctions of eBay-specific software, and discovered that one could buy plug-ins that automated the bidding process.

This bothered me. I thought about it. It bothered me more.

The idea of this software ran entirely counter to the peculiar psychology of bidding at auction. The software-driven sniper isn't really bidding; he's shopping. Skimming an existing situation. The sniper (or his software package) is able to look at the final minutes of any auction as a done deal, then decide whether or not to purchase that item at the fixed price, plus one bid increment. Which pissed me off, and took some of the fun away.

A friend's hacker boyfriend, in Chicago, offered to write me a piece of software that would outsnipe anything on the market. Tempting, but not very. Instead, I sent eBay a message to the effect that allowing autobid software detracted from the eBay experience. That it spoiled the chemistry of the thing, which in my view was a large part of what they offered as a venue. I also suspected, though I couldn't think of a convincing way to put it, that sufficient proliferation of sniping software could eventually, theoretically, bring the whole community to a halt.

I got no reply, and I hadn't expected to, but the problem seems in the meantime to have been resolved. Entirely to my satisfaction, and in a way that illustrates exactly how things have a way of finding their own uses for the street.

Text of a message sent to all vendors of third-party bidding software at eBay, 8/13/98:

> eBay bid system change: Yesterday, through the help of an eBay user, we detected and disarmed a "bid bot" which had placed bids on hundreds of items. A bid bot is a program which bids on many items or the same item over and over again. Our SafeHarbour team is tracking down the source of the bot, and will be working with our lawyers and the authorities to take appropriate action. In an effort to prevent this type of system attack in the future, eBay plans to make an internal change to the bidding process. Most of you will not notice this change. It will NOT affect the interface you use at all. All bidding processes will remain the same as they were before. Unfortunately, the change may disable most, if not all "automated bidding programs" [aka, sniping programs]. We apologize for this, but it's important that we make eBay safe from robots of this kind.

I'd love to know what that bot was bidding on. Beanie Babies, probably. (A follow-up message partially reversed course: eBay would not outlaw bid bots, but would require that they conform to sign-on procedures.)

With a level playing field restored, I decided to kick this eBay watch-buying habit in the head.

Addictive personality that I am, I decided that the best way to do that was to binge: to do a whole bunch of it at one time and get it out of my system. To that end, I decided to buy a couple of fairly serious watches. Keepers.

I bid on, and won, a late-1940s Jaeger two-register chronograph in Hong Kong. The idea of sending a check off to Causeway Bay for more than a thousand dollars to someone I'd never heard of, let alone met, seemed to be stretching it a little. But Eric So, a B Tech (Mech) at the Hong Kong Water Supplies Department and an avid watch fancier, was so evidently honest, so helpful, and responded to e-mail so readily, that I soon had no reservations whatever. Once the check had cleared, the Jaeger arrived with blinding speed and was even nicer than described.

And I did have one authentic auction-frisson over the Jaeger when, very near the end of the auction, someone bidding "by hand" topped me. This gentleman, when I checked his profile, appeared to be a European collector of some seriousness. After I bid again, I waited nervously, but he never came back.

My other binge watch was a Vulcain Cricket, an alarm watch introduced in the late Forties, which sounds like a very large, very mechanical cricket. I wanted one of these because the older ones look terrific, and because "Vulcain Cricket" is one of the finest pieces of found poetry I've ever stumbled across.

I found the best one I'd ever seen, offered by Vince and Laura, of Good Timing, who, by virtue of tagging all their items "(GOOD TIMING)," have built themselves the equivalent of a stall in cyberspace. Most sellers' goods on eBay are spread, as it were, on the same huge blanket, but Vince and Laura's tag allows them an edge in rep-building.

I think it worked, the binge cure. Possibly because getting serious about choosing serious watches made the shuffling of pages a chore rather than a pleasure. Whereas before I'd been able to veg out, in the style of watching some version of the Shopping Channel that actually interested me, I now felt as though I were buying real estate. Investing. Collecting.

I'd always hoped that I wouldn't turn into the sort of person who collected anything.

I no longer open to watches on eBay first thing in the morning. Days go by without my contributing so much as a single hit.

Or maybe I just have enough wristwatches.

I wonder, though, at the extent to which eBay facilitated my passage through this particular consumer obsession. Into it and out the other side in a little under a year. How long would it have taken me to get up to speed on vintage watches without eBay? Would I have started attending watch shows? Would I have had to travel? Would it have taken years? Would I have gotten into it at all?

Probably not.

In Istanbul, one chill misty morning in 1970, I stood in Kapali Carsi, the grand bazaar, under a Sony sign bristling with alien futurity, and stared deep into a cube of plate glass filled with tiny, ancient, fascinating things.

Hanging in that ancient venue, a place whose onsite café, I was told, had been open, twenty-four hours a day, three hundred and sixty-five days a year, literally for centuries, the Sony sign—very large, very proto-*Blade Runner*, illuminated in some way I hadn't seen before—made a deep impression. I'd been living on a Greek island, an archaeological protectorate where cars were prohibited, vacationing in the past.

The glass cube was one man's shop. He was a dealer in curios, and from within it he would reluctantly fetch, like the human equivalent of those robotic cranes in amusement arcades, objects I indicated that I wished to examine. He used a long pair of spring-loaded faux-ivory chopsticks, antiques themselves, their warped tips lent traction by wrappings of rubber bands.

And with these he plucked up, and I purchased, a single stone bead of great beauty, the color of apricot, with bright mineral blood at its core, to make a necklace for the girl I'd later marry, and an excessively mechanical Swiss cigarette lighter, circa 1911 or so, broken, its hallmarked silver case crudely soldered with strange, Eastern, aftermarket sigils.

And in that moment, I think, were all the elements of a real futurity: all the elements of the world toward which we were heading—an emerging technology, a map that was about to evert, to swallow the territory it represented. The technology that sign foreshadowed would become the venue, the city itself. And the bazaar within it.

But I'm glad we still have a place for things to change hands. Even here, in this territory the map became.

Gosh, but could this article ever do with a haircut. It's at least twice as long as it needs to be: dripping with wholly extraneous detail. I must have had really quite a lot of coffee. Sorry about that. Although it does detail my mysteriously belated arrival in cyberspace, should anyone ever be interested, while forever proving how little I actually knew (or know) about any of that stuff.

I had very little idea of what I was talking about, when I wrote this. This tends to be the case when I discuss newly emergent technologies, and is always the case when one makes generalizations about depths of specialist knowledge one is still scarcely aware of. I stood, at the time of writing this, unknowingly, on a precipice. I was about to learn quite a bit about vintage watches. To the extent that I think I can now honestly say that I've forgotten more about vintage watches than I currently know. This overlong, over-caffeinated piece was mainly an expression of that, of excitement at the start of a long, steep, delightfully unnecessary learning curve.

People who've read this piece often assume that I subsequently became a collector of watches. I didn't, at least not in my own view. Collections of things, and their collectors, have generally tended to give me the willies. I sometimes, usually only temporarily, accumulate things in some one category, but the real pursuit is in the learning curve. The dive into esoterica. The quest for expertise. This one lasted, in its purest form, for five or six years. None of the eBay purchases documented here proved to be "keepers." Not even close.

As it happened, I wound up buying and selling quite a few old watches, and bits and pieces of old watches, an activity that gradually introduced to me a peculiarly various global crew of actual über-experts. It was . . . Pynchonian! I never found Lot 49, but I did meet at least two guys who claim to have been there when it sold (one of whom believed it to have been a clever forgery, christened up from parts of two others). Really quite deeply and wonderfully weird, and resulting in some lasting and highly enjoyable friendships.

Today I own no more watches than fingers, and am gradually but actively de-acquisitioning (watches, please, not fingers) so I am pleased to assume that I've cleared the virus.

MY OWN PRIVATE TOKYO

WIRED
SEPTEMBER 2001

I WISH I HAD A THOUSAND-YEN note for every journalist who, over the past decade, has asked me whether Japan is still as futurologically sexy as it seemed to be in the Eighties. If I did, I'd take one of these spotlessly lace-upholstered taxis over to the Ginza and buy my wife a small box of the most expensive Belgian chocolates in the universe.

I'm back to Tokyo tonight to refresh my sense of place, check out the post-Bubble city, professionally resharpen that handy Japanese edge. If you believe, as I do, that all cultural change is essentially technology-driven, you pay attention to Japan. There are reasons for that, and they run deep.

Dining late, in a plastic-draped gypsy noodle stall in Shinjuku, the classic cliché better-than-*Blade Runner* Tokyo street set, I scope my neighbor's phone as he checks his text messages. Wafer-thin, Kandy Kolor pearlescent white, complexly curvilinear, totally ephemeral looking, its screen seethes with a miniature version of Shinjuku's neon light show. He's got the rosary-like anticancer charm attached; most people here do, believing it deflects microwaves, grounding them away from the brain. It looks great, in terms of a novelist's need for props, but it may not actually be that next-generation in terms of what I'm used to back home.

Tokyo has been my handiest prop shop for as long as I've been writing: sheer eye candy. You can see more chronological strata of futuristic design in a Tokyo streetscape than anywhere else in the world. Like successive layers of Tomorrowlands, older ones showing through when the newer ones start to peel.

So the pearlescent phone with the cancer thingy gets drafted straight into props, but what about Japan itself? The Bubble's gone, successive economic plans sputter and wobble to the same halt, one political scandal follows another. . . . Is that the future?

Yes. Part of it, and not necessarily ours, but definitely yes. The Japanese love "futuristic" things precisely because they've been living in the future for such a very long time now. History, that other form of speculative fiction, explains why.

The Japanese, you see, have been repeatedly drop-kicked, ever further down the timeline, by serial national traumata of quite unthinkable weirdness, by a hundred and fifty years of deep, almost constant, change. The twentieth century, for Japan, was like a ride on a rocket sled, with successive bundles of fuel igniting spontaneously, one after another.

They have had one strange ride, the Japanese, and we tend to forget that.

IN 1854, with Commodore Perry's second landing, gunboat diplomacy ended two hundred years of self-imposed isolation, a deliberate stretching out of the feudal dream-time. The Japanese knew that America, not to be denied, had come knocking with the future in its hip pocket. This was the quintessential cargo-cult moment for Japan: the arrival of alien tech.

The people who ran Japan—the emperor, the lords and ladies of his court, the nobles, and the very wealthy—were entranced. It must have seemed as though these visitors emerged from some rip in the fabric of reality. Imagine the Roswell Incident as a trade mission, a successful one; imagine us buying all the Gray technology we could afford, no reverse engineering required. This was a cargo cult where the cargo actually did what it claimed to do.

They must all have gone briefly but thoroughly mad, then pulled it together somehow and plunged on. The Industrial Revolution came whole, in kit form: steamships, railroads, telegraphy, factories, western medicine, the division of labor—not to mention a mechanized military and the political will to use it. Then those Americans returned to whack Asia's first industrial society with the light of a thousand suns—twice, and very hard—and thus the War ended.

At which point the aliens arrived in force, this time with briefcases and plans, bent on a cultural retrofit from the scorched earth up. Certain central aspects of the feudal-industrial core were left intact, while other areas of the nation's political and business culture were heavily grafted with American tissue, resulting in hybrid forms. . . .

HERE IN my Akasaka hotel, I can't sleep. I get dressed and walk to Roppongi, through a not-unpleasantly humid night in the shadows of an exhaust-stained multilevel expressway that feels like the oldest thing in town.

Roppongi is an interzone, the land of *gaijin* bars, always up late. I'm waiting at a pedestrian crossing when I see her. She's probably Australian, young and quite serviceably beautiful. She wears very expensive, very sheer black undergarments, and little else, save for some black outer layer—equally sheer, skintight, and micro-short—and some gold and diamonds to give potential clients the right idea. She steps past me, into four lanes of traffic, conversing on her phone in urgent Japanese. Traffic halts obediently for this triumphantly jaywalking *gaijin* in her black suede spikes. I watch her make the opposite curb, the brain-cancer deflector on her slender little phone swaying in counterpoint to her hips. When the light changes, I cross, and watch her high-five a bouncer who looks like Oddjob in a Paul Smith suit, his skinny lip beard razored with micrometer precision. There's a flash of white as their palms meet. Folded paper. Junkie origami.

This ghost of the Bubble, this reminder of Tokyo from when it was the lodestar for every hustler on the face of the planet, strolls on and then ducks into a doorway near the Sugar Heel Bondage Bar. I last came here right on the cusp of that era, just before the downturn, when her kind were legion. She's old-school, this girl: *fin de siècle* Tokyo decadence. A nostalgia piece.

The Bubble, I think, walking back to the hotel with a box of sushi and a bottle of Bikkle from a high-end liquor store, that was their next-to-last kick. That transplanted postwar American industrial tissue took a while, and in the Eighties it finally did the trick, but the economic jet fuel couldn't be sustained.

The world's second-richest economy, after nearly a decade of stagflation (the century's final kick), still looks like the world's richest place, but energies have shifted, global ley lines of money and hustle have invisibly realigned, yet it feels to me as though all that crazy momentum has finally arrived. Somewhere. Here. Under the expressway Andrei Tarkovsky used for a sci-fi set when he shot *Solaris*.

NEXT DAY, I run into fellow Vancouverite Douglas Coupland in the Shibuya branch of Tokyu Hands, an eight-floor DIY emporium where doing it yourself includes things like serious diamond-cutting. He introduces me to Michael Stipe. Coupland is as jet-lagged as I am, but Stipe indicates that he's actually club-lagged, having stayed up till two in the morning the night before. And how does he like Tokyo? "It rocks," says Stipe.

Later, having headed for Harajuku and Kiddy Land, another eight floors—these devoted to toys that definitely aren't us—I find myself distracted outside Harajuku Station by a bevy of teenage manga nurses, rocker girls kitted out in knee-high black platform boots, black jodhpurs, black Lara Croft tops, and open, carefully starched lab coats, stethoscopes around their necks.

The look clearly isn't happening without a stethoscope.

They're doing the Harajuku hang—smoking cigarettes, talking on their little phones, and being seen. I circle them for a while, hoping one will have a colostomy bag or a Texas catheter worked into her outfit, but the look, like most looks here or anywhere, is rigidly delineated. They all have the same black lipstick, worn away to pink at the center.

I think about the nurses on my way back to the hotel. Something about dreams, about the interface between the private and the consensual. You can do that here, in Tokyo: be a teenage girl on the street in a bondage-nurse outfit. You can dream in public. And the reason you can do it is that this is one of the safest cities in the world, and a special zone, Harajuku, has already been set aside for you. That was true during the Bubble, and remains true today, in the face of drugs and slackers and a notable local increase in globalization. The Japanese, in the course of being booted down the timeline, have learned to keep it together in ways that we're only just starting to imagine. They don't really worry, not the way we do. The manga nurses don't threaten anything; there's a place for them, and for whatever replaces them.

I SPEND my last night in Shinjuku with Coupland and a friend. It's hard to beat, these nameless neon streets swarming with every known form of electronic advertising, under a misting rain that softens the commercials playing on façade screens of quite surreal width and clarity. The Japanese know this about television: Make it big enough and anything looks cool.

Those French Situationists, going on about the Society of the Spectacle, they didn't have a clue. This is it, right here, and I love it. Shinjuku at night is one of the most deliriously beautiful places in the world, and somehow the silliest of all beautiful places—and the combination is sheer delight.

And tonight, watching the Japanese do what they do here, amid all this electric kitsch, all this randomly overlapped media, this chaotically stable neon storm of marketing hoopla, I've got my answer: Japan is still the future, and if the vertigo is gone, it really only means that they've made it out the far end of that tunnel of prematurely accelerated change. Here, in the first city to have this firmly and this comfortably arrived in this new century—the most truly contemporary city on earth—the center is holding.

In a world of technologically driven exponential change, the Japanese have an acquired edge: They know how to live with it. Nobody legislates that kind of change into being, it just comes, and keeps coming, and the Japanese have been experiencing it for more than a hundred years.

I see them poised here tonight, hanging out, life going on, in the glow of these very big televisions. Postgraduates at all of this.

Home at last, in the twenty-first century.

Rereading this makes me feel I owe Wired *an article about Tokyo.*

Not so much because I shamelessly, if less eloquently, re-hash the best part of the Observer *piece you may already have read here, but because of a weird internal conflict, at the time, between fiction and non. All of the good stuff I encountered in*

Tokyo, that time (aside from the Australian girl crossing the street) got siphoned off, exclusively, into Pattern Recognition, *the novel I was writing at the time. Cayce's Tokyo, in* Pattern Recognition, *is the Tokyo I encountered, at* Wired's *considerable expense. None of which I was able to access for* Wired. *Just not possible. The fiction-writing space was occupied, this time, and my very cursory showing, in this piece, is the result of my having had no place, within myself, to do the work required. Really I should have found a way to spot-weld on some inner sidewalk, but all I managed to do was something that feels to me, in the end, literally phoned in.*

THE ROAD TO OCEANIA

THE NEW YORK TIMES

JUNE 2003

WALKING ALONG Henrietta Street recently, by London's Covent Garden, looking for a restaurant, I found myself thinking of George Orwell. Victor Gollancz Ltd., publisher of Orwell's early work, had its offices there in 1984, when they published my first novel, a novel of an imagined future.

At the time, I felt I had lived most of my life under the looming shadow of that mythic year—Orwell having found his title by inverting the final digits of the year of his book's completion. It seemed very strange to actually be alive in 1984. In retrospect, I think it has seemed stranger even than living in the twenty-first century.

I had a valuable secret in 1984, though, one I owed in large part to Orwell, who would have turned 100 today: I knew that the novel I had written wasn't really about the future, just as *1984* hadn't been about the future, but about 1948. I had relatively little anxiety about eventually finding myself in a society of the sort Orwell imagined. I had other fish to fry, in terms of history and anxiety, and indeed I still do.

Today, on Henrietta Street, one sees the rectangular housings of closed-circuit television cameras, angled watchfully down from shop fronts. Orwell might have seen these as something out of Jeremy Bentham, the utilitarian philosopher, penal theorist, and spiritual father of the panoptic project of surveillance. But for me they posed stranger possibilities, the street itself seeming to have evolved sensory apparatus in the service of some meta-project beyond any imagining of the closed-circuit system's designers.

Orwell knew the power of the press, our first mass medium, and at the BBC he'd witnessed the first electronic medium (radio) as it was brought to bear on wartime public opinion. He died before broadcast television had come into its own, but had he lived I doubt that anything about it would have much surprised him. The media of *1984* are broadcast technology imagined in the service of a totalitarian state, and no different from the media of Saddam Hussein's Iraq or of North Korea today—technologically backward societies in which information is still mostly broadcast. Indeed, today, reliance on broadcasting is the very definition of a technologically backward society.

Elsewhere, driven by the acceleration of computing power and connectivity and the simultaneous development of surveillance systems and tracking technologies, we are approaching a theoretical state of absolute informational transparency, one in which "Orwellian" scrutiny is no longer a strictly hierarchical, top-down activity, but to some extent a democratized one. As individuals steadily lose degrees of privacy, so too do corporations and states. Loss of traditional privacies may seem in the short term to be driven by issues of national security, but this may prove in time to have been intrinsic to the nature of ubiquitous information.

Certain goals of the government's Total (now Terrorist) Information Awareness initiative may eventually be realized simply by the evolution of the global information system—but not necessarily or exclusively for the benefit of the United States or any other government. This outcome may be an inevitable result of the migration to cyberspace of everything that we do with information.

Had Orwell known that computers were coming (out of Bletchley Park, oddly, a dilapidated English country house, home to the pioneering efforts of Alan Turing and other wartime code-breakers) he might have imagined a Ministry of Truth empowered by punch cards and vacuum tubes to better wring the last vestiges of freedom from the population of Oceania. But I doubt his story would have been very different. Would East Germany's Stasi have been saved if its agents had been able to mouse away on PC's into the Nineties? The system would still have been crushed. It just wouldn't have been under the weight of paper surveillance.

Orwell's projections come from the era of information broadcasting, and are not applicable to our own. Had Orwell been able to equip Big Brother with all the tools of artificial intelligence, he would still have been writing from an older paradigm, and the result could never have described our situation today, nor suggested where we might be heading.

That our own biggish brothers, in the name of national security, draw from ever wider and increasingly transparent fields of data may disturb us, but this is something that corporations, nongovernmental organizations and individuals do as well, with greater and greater frequency. The collection and management of information, at every level, is exponentially empowered by the global nature of the system itself, a system unfettered by national boundaries or, increasingly, government control.

It is becoming unprecedentedly difficult for anyone, anyone at all, to keep a secret.

In the age of the leak and the blog, of evidence extraction and link discovery, truths will either out or be outed, later if not sooner. This is something I would bring to the attention of every diplomat, politician, and corporate leader: The future, eventually, will find you out. The future, wielding unimaginable tools of transparency, will have its way with you. In the end, you will be seen to have done that which you did.

I say "truths," however, and not "truth," as the other side of information's new ubiquity can look not so much transparent as outright crazy. Regardless of the number and power of the tools used to extract patterns from information, any sense of meaning depends on context, with interpretation coming along in support of one agenda or another. A world of informational transparency will necessarily be one of deliriously multiple viewpoints, shot through with misinformation, disinformation, conspiracy theories and a quotidian degree of madness. We may be able to see what's going on more quickly, but that doesn't mean we'll agree about it any more readily.

Orwell did the job he set out to do, did it forcefully and brilliantly, in the painstaking creation of our best-known dystopia. I've seen it said that because he chose to go there, as rigorously and fearlessly as he did, we don't have to. I like to think there's some truth in that. But the ground of history has a way of shifting the most basic of assumptions from beneath the most scrupulously imagined situations. Dystopias are no more real than utopias. None of us ever really inhabits either—except, in the case of dystopias, in the relative and ordinarily tragic sense of life in some extremely unfortunate place.

This is not to say that Orwell failed in any way, but rather that he succeeded. *Nineteen Eighty-Four* remains one of the quickest and most succinct routes to the core realities of 1948. If you wish to know an era, study its most lucid nightmares. In the mirrors of our darkest fears, much will be revealed. But don't mistake those mirrors for road maps to the future, or even to the present.

We've missed the train to Oceania, and live today with stranger problems.

I do still trust that somewhere down the line, closer to full-on Borgesian digital singularity, pretty much all will have eventually been revealed.

In the meantime, though, the thought in this piece that seems to me to have been most meaningfully predictive of that meantime is that the digital is also an ominously perfect medium for the propagation of all manner of conspiracy theories and "alternate truths." We have certainly seen a lot of that, since the centenary of Orwell's birth, and in ways that I imagine would have concerned Orwell.

This idea, of the digital's simultaneous tendency to increase transparency while increasing craziness, wasn't mine. I encountered it in the Global Business Network's 2003 Scenario Book, History in Motion. *I have been a grateful if largely inactive member of GBN since shortly after its founding, as membership has brought many new and often crucial ideas into my fiction-writing space. GBN used to have the loveliest imaginable free book club for members, as well as the loveliest possible cardboard shipping cartons, in which I still store my manuscripts. Thank you, GBN, for having allowed me to be a wallflower all these years.*

SKIP SPENCE'S JEANS

UGLY THINGS

2003

AFTER ALTAMONT, AND THE MANSON MURDERS, with the hot fat of the Sixties congealing in a suddenly cold pan, I flew out to San Jose to visit a couple of acquaintances from D.C. They'd gone there intending to start a band. The one who did start a band was Little John, the original drummer for what became the Doobie Brothers.

I had no idea what San Jose might be like—otherwise I wouldn't have gone there. After an initial horrific foray into what was left of the Haight (I'd missed its heyday, whenever that might have been), I quickly retreated to San Jose. The Haight was a Burroughsian cartoon, a few skeletal speed-driven life-forms scuttling back and forth across streets that had been nuked by the Methedrine Bomb. San Jose, on the other hand, was the dullest blue-collar bohemia imaginable, an utterly style-free zone in which the local bikers displayed the nearest thing to panache. The pot came sprayed with PCP, the wrong kind of excitement. It was dull as ditchwater, aside from being vaguely dangerous; so dull that I began to fear I'd get depressed enough to stay there.

One evening, though, just at dusk, I went out for a stroll with Little John and two other denizens of what would later, after my departure, become Chez Doobie. A block or so from the house, an astonishing figure appeared. Tall, very handsome, and quite magically elegant, this apparition was introduced to me as Skip Spence, formerly of Moby Grape.

His outfit was the single most perfect expression of Country Music Hip I'd ever seen, and I've seen nothing to match it since. Nothing Nudie about it, nothing Flying Burrito, but, rather, classic-with-a-twist, rooted in the kind of hardcore rodeo esoterica I'd glimpsed a little of during my school years in Tucson. His jacket may have been Filson, the Seattle outfitter, something in a riding twill, but a western business cut, not casual. Under this, he wore a white pinpoint oxford Supima (these are always Supima) cotton western business shirt, buttoned at the collar, no tie. His hat, well, I knew enough about cowboy hats to know that I knew nothing about them, but I guessed that this one was on par with the rest of his outfit. (He removed it while he spoke with us, holding it carefully and rather formally.) His boots, I guessed, were not Tony Lama but by someone whose clients could only smile patiently at the mention of Tony Lama. But between jacket and jeans stretched a long-legged vertical of dark indigo denim, and this is what made the strongest and most lasting impression. Skip Spence's jeans were perfect. As I stared at them, while he and the ur-Doobies chatted gravely about studios and managers, I understood: They were a pair of Levi's, likely several sizes too large to begin with, which had been deconstructed, a seam at a time, then meticulously tailored, each seam perfectly resewn with the correct iodine-tint thread. But not only did they fit him exquisitely, as perfectly as garment has ever fit man—they had been reconstructed, recontextualized, jacked out of blue denim mundania entirely, into some unknown realm of Hispano-American, deeply Catholic romanticism.

They fell over his boots without a break, by virtue of the fronts having been slit, the edges perfectly hemmed, and, down front and back, creases had been sewn in. They would have to be dry-cleaned, I decided, itself a novel concept, then, when it came to jeans.

He had all the style of someone from another and better planet, in that working-class northern California residential street, but I knew that I was experiencing star quality, and that he would've gone as easily off the scale on the Kings Road.

And then he said goodbye, and we walked on, and someone allowed, quietly, that Skip had a problem with heroin, and that there were problems with his label. But, they all agreed, he was a good guy, a very good guy indeed, and that he had promised to help them. And I imagine that he did.

I never forgot him, and the gift of his brave elegance, and it was only a year or so ago that I heard *Oar* for the first time.

Skip Spence's album Oar *is a fine and touching and deeply other thing. Offhand, my favorite example of quite clinically outsider art. It still amazes me that it took me decades to hear it.*

TERMINAL CITY

INTRODUCTION TO PHANTOM SHANGHAI,
PHOTOGRAPHS BY GREG GIRARD

2007

I'VE NEVER HAD quite this difficult a time before, trying to think of something to say at the front of a book. I've had a box of prints of Greg Girard's photographs here for entirely too long now, and every time I open it, and start looking through them, it's as though my head falls off.

I've never seen anything like them. I have, though, imagined things not unlike what they depict, though never at anything like this resolution. In my novel *Neuromancer*, when the protagonists visit a decrepit surviving fragment of lower Manhattan, hemmed in by my sketchy description of Bigger, Globally Corporate Things, I had something like these photographs in mind.

But really, every time I open the box and look at them, they shut me up. Lump in throat.

Liminal. Images at the threshold. Of the threshold. The dividing line. Something slicing across accretions of cultural memory like Buñuel's razor.

Documents of the Gone World, captured, one thinks, the Tuesday before it went entirely. Something so aching. The record of something which we know, instinctively, shouldn't happen. They really shouldn't do this, but . . .

Erasure. And look what they've erased. Wiped clean. Catch

this last (and in my case, first) glimpse. Adios. "One little whoops and a push." Gone, then.

And beyond the shattered matchstick fields of progress arise these shoals of cheap-ass concrete thunderheads, these arc-lit mesas apparently designed to emulate downmarket Japanese consumer electronics.

At the time of this writing, I freely confess, I know little more about Shanghai than these images. They came upon me, as it were, in the night, unexpectedly.

I know, and knew instantly, that I will never forget them.

I had long treasured Ian Lambot and Greg Girard's *City of Darkness*, but in its case I had already seen other, and as it happened quite splendid, photographs of Hak Nam, and knew that that place, that near-infinitely interstitial universe or black hole, was indeed Gone.

Phantom Shanghai is the actual vanishing, the hideous twenty-first-century urban hat-trick itself. I think of the line of dawn rushing through desert, causing stones to explode. It is almost more than I can bear to contemplate, though the images themselves are so gorgeous, so extraordinary, that of course I look and look.

These images truly are, in that particular coinage of J. G. Ballard's, terminal documents. One might compare them to Robert Polidori's images of Pripyat and Chernobyl, except that what Girard reveals is so much more possibly the fate of so many places, hence so much more terrible.

I go back to the box, look again, and again am struck silent.

"Pictures or it didn't happen," they say on the Internet.

One of Greg Girard's pictures is worth some ridiculously high number of my words. If you want to have an unforgettable experience, find this book and see why I was rendered basically speechless.

"Terminal City" was some rail magnate's early suggestion for naming Vancouver. It's a very lazy title for this introduction. I wish I'd thought of something better.

INTRODUCTION: "THE BODY"

INTRODUCTION TO STELARC: THE MONOGRAPH,

MARQUARD SMITH, EDITOR

2005

THERE WAS A HEYDAY of virtual reality conferences during the late Eighties and early Nineties, and thus I found myself in Barcelona, San Francisco, Tokyo, or Linz, blinking through jet-lag at various manifestations of new technology, art, and attempts at interfacing the two. Very little of this stuff managed to work its way into long-term memory, most of it evaporating from the buffer almost immediately. Highly memorable, though, were the destructo-displays of Survival Research Laboratories, the machine-assisted street theater of Barcelona's La Fura dels Baus, and the performances of Stelarc.

When eventually I was able to meet Stelarc himself, in Melbourne, I found that he radiated a most remarkable calm and amiability, as though the extraordinary adventures he'd put "the body" through had somehow freed him of the ordinary levels of anxiety most of us experience.

As he sat in a Melbourne restaurant, recalling the sensation of having discovered that a robotic "sculpture," inserted down his throat and mechanically unfurled, was stubbornly refusing to refurl for removal, and that surgical intervention might shortly be the only option, he struck me as one of the calmest people I'd ever met. He resembled a younger J. G. Ballard, it seemed to me, another utterly conventional-looking man whose deeply unconventional ideas have taken him to singular destinations. Ballard's destinations, however, have been fictional, and Stelarc's are often physical, and sometimes seem to include the possibility of terminality (as with the elegant little sculpture converting "the body" to gallery space).

I had first encountered this art in the pages of the American magazine *ReSearch*: photographs of an event in which unbarbed steel hooks were inserted through various parts of "the body." Counterbalanced with rocks, on ropes, these then levitated the prone body, which remained suspended for some period of time above the heads of onlookers. This immediately put Stelarc on my map. Who was this person, and what was he up to? Whatever it was, I sensed that it had little to do with rest of the magazine's contents (someone who'd opted to bifurcate his penis, extremes of recreational corsetry, etc.).

Later, at the Art Futura festival in Barcelona, I saw video footage of more robotically oriented Stelarc performances. I imagine now that I was watching Stelarc in performance with his robotic third arm, but what I recall experiencing was a vision of some absolute chimera, at the heart of a labyrinth of breathtaking complexity. I sensed that the important thing wasn't the entity Stelarc evoked, but the labyrinth that the creature's manifestation suggested.

Extraordinary images, not least because they seemed the literal physical realization of Marcel Duchamp's *Nude Descending a Staircase, No. 2.*

Stelarc's art has never seemed "futuristic" to me. If I felt it were, I doubt I'd have responded to it. Rather, I experience it in a context that includes circuses, freak shows, medical museums, the passions of solitary inventors. I associate it with Leonardo da Vinci's ornithopter, eccentric nineteenth-century velocipedes, and Victorian schemes for electroplating the dead. Though not retrograde in any way: timeless, as though each performance constitutes a moment equivalent to those collected in Humphrey Jennings's *Pandaemonium: The Coming of the Machine* in the Industrial Revolution: moments of the purest technologically induced cognitive disjunction.

I am delighted at the publication of this volume, and look forward to a day when the world's museums house effectively immortal suburbs of that great work, "the body."

Stelarc walks the Posthumanist talk.

THE NET IS A
WASTE OF TIME

THE NEW YORK TIMES MAGAZINE

JULY 1996

I COINED THE WORD "cyberspace" in 1981 in one of my first science-fiction stories and subsequently used it to describe something that people insist on seeing as a sort of literary forerunner of the Internet. This being so, some think it remarkable that I do not use e-mail. In all truth, I have avoided it because I am lazy and enjoy staring blankly into space (which is also the space where novels come from) and because unanswered mail, e- or otherwise, is a source of discomfort.

But I have recently become an avid browser of the World Wide Web. Some people find this odd. My wife finds it positively perverse. I, however, scent big changes afoot, possibilities that were never quite as manifest in earlier incarnations of the Net.

I was born in 1948. I can't recall a world before television, but I know I must have experienced one. I do, dimly, recall the arrival of a piece of brown wooden furniture with sturdy Bakelite knobs and a screen no larger than the screen on this PowerBook.

Initially there was nothing on it but "snow," and then the nightly advent of a targetlike device called "the test pattern," which people actually gathered to watch.

Today I think about the test pattern as I surf the Web. I imagine that the World Wide Web and its modest wonders are no more than the test pattern for whatever the twenty-first century will regard as its equivalent medium. Not that I can even remotely imagine what that medium might actually be.

In the age of wooden television in the South where I grew up, leisure involved sitting on screened porches, smoking cigarettes, drinking iced tea, engaging in conversation, and staring into space. It might also involve fishing.

Sometimes the Web does remind me of fishing. It never reminds me of conversation, although it can feel a lot like staring into space. "Surfing the Web" (as dubious a metaphor as "the information highway") is, as a friend of mind has it, "like reading magazines with the pages stuck together." My wife shakes her head in dismay as I patiently await the downloading of some Japanese Beatles fan's personal catalog of bootlegs. "But it's from Japan!" She isn't moved. She goes out to enjoy the flowers in her garden.

I stay in. Hooked. Is this leisure—this browsing, randomly linking my way through these small patches of virtual real-estate—or do I somehow imagine that I am performing some more dynamic function? The content of the Web aspires to absolute variety. One might find anything there. It is like rummaging in the forefront of the collective global mind. Somewhere, surely, there is a site that contains . . . everything we have lost?

The finest and most secret pleasure afforded new users of the Web rests in submitting to the search engine of AltaVista the names of people we may not have spoken aloud in years. Will she be here? Has he survived unto this age? (She isn't there. Someone with his name has recently posted to a news group concerned with gossip about soap stars.) What is this casting of the nets of identity? Do we engage here in something of a tragic seriousness?

In the age of wooden television, media were there to entertain, to sell an advertiser's product, perhaps to inform. Watching television, then, could indeed be considered a leisure activity. In our hypermediated age, we have come to suspect that watching television constitutes a species of work. Postindustrial creatures of an information economy, we increasingly sense that accessing media is what we do. We have become terminally self-conscious. There is no such thing as simple entertainment. We watch ourselves watching. We watch ourselves watching Beavis and Butt-Head, who are watching rock videos. Simply to watch without the buffer of irony in place, might reveal a fatal naïveté.

But that is our response to aging media like film and television, survivors from the age of wood. The Web is new, and our response to it has not yet hardened. That is a large part of its appeal. It is something half-formed, growing. Larval. It is not what it was six months ago; in another six months it will be something else again. It was not planned; it simply happened, is happening. It is happening the way cities happened. It is a city.

Toward the end of the age of wooden televisions, the futurists of the Sunday supplements announced the advent of the "leisure society." Technology would leave us less and less to do in the Marxian sense of yanking the levers of production. The challenge, then, would be to fill our days with meaningful, healthful, satisfying activity. As with most products of an earlier era's futurism, we find it difficult today to imagine the exact coordinates from which this vision came. In any case, our world does not offer us a surplus of leisure. The word itself has grown somehow suspect, as quaint and vaguely melancholy as the battered leather valise in a Ralph Lauren window display. Only the very old or the economically disadvantaged (provided they are not chained to the schedules of their environment's more demanding addictions) have a great deal of time on their hands. To be successful, apparently, is to be chronically busy. As new technologies search out and lace over every interstice in the net of global communication, we find ourselves with increasingly less excuse for . . . slack.

And that, I would argue, is what the World Wide Web, the test pattern for whatever will become the dominant global medium, offers us. Today, in its clumsy, larval, curiously innocent way, it offers us the opportunity to waste time, to wander aimlessly, to daydream about the countless other lives, the other people, on the far sides of however many monitors in that post-geographical meta-country we increasingly call home. It will probably evolve into something considerably less random, and less fun—we seem to have a knack for that—but in the meantime, in its gloriously unsorted Global Ham Television Postcard Universes phase, surfing the Web is a procrastinator's dream. And people who see you doing it might even imagine you're working.

"... *the search engine of AltaVista*"? *Blimey. Spoken from a pre-Google universe. A tender and unformed time indeed.*

For all of that, though, when I read this now I think that what I should more accurately have called the Web did become what I expected it to. Though in the way of these things, it became so much else as well.

TIME MACHINE CUBA

INFINITE MATRIX

JANUARY 2006

I LEARNED OF SCIENCE FICTION and history in a single season.

History I found in the basement of an old brick house I happened to pass each day, on my way to elementary school, in a small town in Virginia.

This house stood vacant, but was in too conspicuous a state of repair to seem haunted, and had never interested me. One afternoon, though, I noted that workmen had arrived, and that some sort of renovation was being prepared for. Squeezing in past a sheet of plywood, I explored a series of cold, empty rooms. One of these (my heart beat faster) contained a damp old trunk. Having worked up the nerve to open it, I found only a few faded lithographs (as I now imagine they were) of airplanes. But these were airplanes unlike any I had seen, and they held my attention in a peculiar way. They were old, clearly of some other era, but exciting, and somehow frightening as well. Squatting there, staring at them, I felt as though some enormous wedge of information was being driven into my head. Various bits and pieces of half-knowledge were coming together, forming some new and utterly unexpected whole. I already knew, as if by osmosis, that there had been a war, though I didn't know when, or with whom. I had been raised, so far, by adults who sometimes spoke of "the war" as some previous time or era or world, but I had somehow never associated that with other, more vague ideas of some past and general conflict. I had read comic books about war, and played with military toys, but had never considered how those might fit into some way the world had actually been.

I had found World War II, in that trunk. I had discovered history, or it me, and I would never be the same.

Science fiction, then, I found on various wire racks, one of them offering a 15-cent copy of the Classics Illustrated version of *The Time Machine*—which must have led me, just as its publishers claimed to have intended it to, to Wells's text. When George Pal's film version was released, in 1960, I already felt, though secretly, that *The Time Machine* was mine, part of a personal and growing collection of alternate universes, and that no one else in the theater really got it.

Even more secretly, I had filled a Blue Horse lined notebook with elaborate pencil sketches for my own, actual, working time machine. It looked, I recall, rather more like the machine in the Classics Illustrated version than the one in George Pal's film. The Classics Illustrated time machine resembled a model of the atom, but I had imagined this, for my own purposes, as geared in some achingly complex spheres-within-spheres way that I could never quite envision in operation, but which would somehow allow it to move in three dimensions at once. That, I imagined, just might do the trick. I suspected, without admitting it to myself, that time travel might be a magic on the order of being able to kiss one's own elbow (which had seemed, initially, to be quite theoretically possible) but I was determined not to admit it. The possibility was too delicious to relinquish.

Although I now think that I had no specific time-travel adventures in mind, no head-scratching paradoxes to be explored. I don't remember dreaming of exploring the past of the world around me, or of journeying to its future.

What I wanted was to attain the world of *The Time Machine*, the Morlocks' garden. Wells's Victorian future nightmare had become a favorite fantasyland, for me. Because it existed so far up the timeline as to be beyond history, and history, once acknowledged, had quickly become a sort of nightmare, one from which there seemed to be no escape.

History, I was learning, there at the start of the 1960s, never stops happening.

I had become an involuntary sponge for modern history, after my discoveries of World War II and science fiction. Much of the science fiction I was reading, American fiction of the 1940s and '50s, had already become history of a sort, requiring an acquired filter for anachronism. I studied the patent Future History timeline Robert Heinlein appended to each of his novels and noted where it began to digress from history as I was coming to know it. I filtered indigestible bits of anachronistic gristle out of this older science fiction, reverse-engineering a model of the real past through a growing understanding of what these authors had gotten wrong.

In another trunk, in my own family attic, I had unearthed World War I. A much more substantial trove, this one: rolled memorial scrolls bearing the names of the hometown dead, and the lightly rusted and altogether astonishing mass of a Colt Model 1911 automatic pistol.

I watched the CBS documentary series *Twentieth Century* on Sunday nights, moved by the eminently sane midwestern voice of Walter Cronkite, as he narrated aspects of the unimaginably complex and peculiar historical reality in which I was learning that I lived. I learned about D-Day, the concentration camps, the atomic bomb, and the Cold War. With these last two, Cronkite's restrained narration met my growing and secret terror at where history and science (or history as science fiction?) seemed almost certainly to be taking us.

And now, walking to school, past the house where I had dis-covered World War II, I passed the post office, newly marked with metal signs bearing the black-and-yellow Civil Defense symbol used to indicate fallout shelters. Sirens were tested regu-larly, along with something called "the system," and the dial of my first transistor radio was marked, twice, with that same sym-bol, indicating the two frequencies set aside for Civil Defense.

Freed by Wells and his literary descendants to roam, in my imagination, up and down the timeline, I had stumbled upon World War III, and the end of civilization.

Wells had discovered the end of civilization long before me. It must have seemed that it kept coming back throughout his life to oppress him, the vision of cataclysm and systemic collapse, fueled by some basic immaturity of the species—to bring an end, at least temporarily, to modern history and technological progress. He must have expected it constantly, through World

Wars I and II. He would have been terribly aware of it looming again, in the years immediately before his death, with the military use of atomic energy an established fact.

In 1905 he had imagined it arriving with the military use of aerial bombs against civilian targets, but then he would see zeppelins bomb London, and after that the Blitz, and then the advent of the German rocket bombs. In *The Time Machine*, wars are a thing of the immemorial past, something necessarily transcended on the way to some safer, more rational basis for society.

None of which mattered to me as I cringed my way through the heating up of the Cold War, expecting any moment the wailing of the sirens that would call us all into the basement of the post office. The television dramatization of Pat Frank's *Alas, Babylon*, a popular novel set in a small Florida town in the immediate aftermath of nuclear war, had sealed my fate. Something akin to Sartre's dictum that hell is other people was dawning on me, and part of the cloud of constant secret terror I inhabited was some conviction that my neighbors, confined in what I imagined as the stifling darkness of a Civil Defense fallout shelter, would prove to be my own personal Morlocks.

The appeal of *The Time Machine* for me, then, became one purely of escape. I longed for Wells's ellipsis, the long blur forward, "night follow[ing] day like the flapping of a black wing." I longed to find myself on the far side of whatever terrible, inevitable history was about to happen. I saw, with utmost clarity, the World War II howitzers, on the town's courthouse lawn, dusted with the falling detritus of Chicago, and the sky above glowing with a new and deadly clarity.

I didn't understand that Wells himself had written a more thorough end to humanity, in *The Time Machine*, than any I imagined descending on America as I knew it. The perversely enjoyable melancholy that pervades the garden of the Eloi emanates not from the hidden underworld of the Morlocks, nor from their grisly symbiosis with their former masters, but from the exquisite and utterly deliberate job of world-wrecking Wells has performed for us. Writers before and after Wells have enjoyed the heady pleasures of reducing the great monuments of their day to imaginary ruin, but few have attained the degree of symbolic elegance, nor the convincingly forlorn realism, of the Palace of Green Porcelain.

The Palace proves to be the ruin of a museum. A single humble box of safety matches, preserved in an airtight glass case, is the treasure the Time Traveler takes with him from that museum of man. A last working token of technology: light and destruction both, in a palm-sized packet. Matches, camphor, and a heavy lever broken from a nameless piece of machinery, to serve as club and pry bar.

He leaves the museum with the tools of his early ancestors: fire and the club.

I had my own ancient tool of destruction, and taught myself, crouching in secret places, to disassemble it, my impossible, scary, secret provision from history. I lightly oiled the parts and hid them separately, wrapped in rags. This being Virginia in the early 1960s, I easily obtained a box of ammunition, alarmingly heavy finger-thick shells with bullets the color of a new copper penny.

I possessed the pistol, it seemed to me, much as the Time Traveler possessed his matches and his makeshift club, though far less purposefully. He leaves the Palace of Green Porcelain with a plan, and I had no plan, only a global and unexpressed terror of impending nuclear war, and of the end of history, and the need to somehow feel in control of something.

Three years into my discovery of history, it was announced that Soviet ballistic missiles had been deployed in Cuba. My encounter with history, I absolutely knew, was about to end then, and perhaps my species with it.

In his preface to the 1921 edition of *The War in the Air*, Wells wrote of World War I (still able to call it, then, the Great War): "The great catastrophe marched upon us in daylight. But everybody thought that somebody else would stop it before it really arrived. Behind that great catastrophe march others today." In his preface to the 1941 edition, he could only add: "Again I ask the reader to note the warnings I gave in that year, twenty years ago. Is there anything to add to that preface now? Nothing except my epitaph. That, when the time comes, will manifestly have to be: 'I told you so. You *damned* fools.' (The italics are mine.)"

The italics are indeed his: the terminally exasperated visionary, the technologically fluent Victorian who has watched the twentieth century arrive, with all of its astonishing baggage of change, and who has come to trust in the minds of the sort of men who ran British Rail. They are the italics of the perpetually impatient and somehow perpetually unworldly futurist, seeing his model going terminally wrong in the hands of the less clever, the less evolved. And they are with us today, those italics, though

I've long since learned to run shy of science fiction that employs them.

I suspect that I began to distrust that particular flavor of italics when the world didn't end in October of 1962. I can't recall the resolution of the Cuban Missile Crisis at all. My anxiety, and the world's, reached some absolute peak. And then declined, history moving on, so much of it, and sometimes today the world of my own childhood strikes me as scarcely less remote than the world of Wells's childhood, so much has changed in the meantime.

I may actually have begun to distrust science fiction, then, or rather to trust it differently, as my initial passion for it began to decline, around that time. I found Henry Miller, then, and William Burroughs, Jack Kerouac, and others, voices of another kind, and the science fiction I continued to read was that which somehow was resonant with those other voices, and where those voices seemed to be leading me.

And it may also have begun to dawn on me, around that same time, that history, though initially discovered in whatever soggy trunk or in whatever caliber, is a species of speculative fiction itself, prone to changing interpretation and further discoveries.

This is a much more directly autobiographical piece than I'm ordinarily prone to, and the result of a failed project. I had been commissioned to write an introduction for a new edition of H. G. Wells's The Time Machine, *and found myself unable to complete it to what I imagined would be the publisher's expectations. It was supposed to be about Wells, not about me, yet this personal narrative kept shouldering aside my not very effective attempts to sound like an academic historian of science fiction (probably because I am so thoroughly not that).*

WILL WE HAVE COMPUTER CHIPS IN OUR HEADS?

TIME
JUNE 19, 2000

MAYBE.

But only once or twice, and probably not for very long.

The cyberpunk hard guys of science fiction, with their sharp black suits and their surgically implanted silicon chips, already have a certain nostalgic romance about them. Information highwaymen, cousins of the "steam bandits" of Victorian techno-fiction: so heroically attuned to the new technology that they have laid themselves open to its very cutting edge. They have become it; they have taken it within themselves.

Meanwhile, in case you somehow haven't noticed, we are all of us becoming it; we seem to have no choice but to take it within ourselves.

In hindsight, the most memorable images of science fiction often have more to do with our anxieties in the past (the writer's present) than with those singular and ongoing scenarios that make up our life as a species: our real futures, our ongoing present.

Many of us, even today, or most particularly today, must feel as though we have silicon chips embedded in our brains. Some of us, certainly, are not entirely happy with that feeling. Some of us must wish that ubiquitous computating would simply go away and leave us alone, a prospect that seems increasingly unlikely.

But that does not, I think, mean that we will one day, as a species, submit to the indignity of the chip. If only because the chip will almost certainly be as quaint an object as the vacuum tube or the slide rule.

From the viewpoint of bioengineering, a silicon chip is a large and rather complex shard of glass. Inserting a silicon chip into the human brain involves a certain irreducible inelegance of scale. It's scarcely more elegant, relatively, than inserting a steam engine into the same tissue. It may be technically possible, but why should we even want to attempt such a thing?

I suspect that medicine and the military will both find reasons for attempting such a thing, at least in the short run, and that medicine's reasons may at least serve to counter someone's acquired or inherited disability. If I were to lose my eyes, I would quite eagerly submit to some sort of surgery promising a video link to the optic nerves (and once there, why not insist on full-channel cable and a Web browser?). The military's reasons for insertion would likely have something to do with what I suspect is the increasingly archaic job description of "fighter pilot," or with some other aspect of telepresent combat, in which weapons in the field are remotely controlled by distant operators. At least there's still a certain macho frisson to be had in the idea of deliberately embedding a tactical shard of glass in one's head, and surely crazier things have been done in the name of king and country.

But if we do do it, I doubt we'll be doing it for very long, as various models of biological and nanomolecular computing are looming rapidly into view. Rather than plug a piece of hardware into our gray matter, how much more elegant to extract some brain cells, plop them into a Petri dish, and graft on various sorts of gelatinous computing goo. Slug it all back into the skull and watch it run on blood sugar, the way a human brain's supposed to. Get all the functions and features you want, without that clunky-junky twentieth-century hardware thing. You really don't need complicated glass to crunch numbers, and computing goo probably won't be all that difficult to build. (The more tricky aspect here may be turning data into something that brain cells understand. If you knew how to make brain cells understand pull-down menus, you'd probably know everything you needed to know about brain cells, period. But we are coming to know, relatively, an awful lot about brain cells.)

Our hardware is likely to turn into something like us a lot faster than we are likely to turn into something like our hardware. Our hardware is evolving at the speed of light, while we are still the product, for the most part, of unskilled labor.

But there is another argument against the need to implant computing devices, be they glass or goo. It's a very simple one, so simple that some have difficulty grasping it. It has to do with a certain archaic distinction we still tend to make, a distinction between computing and "the world." Between, if you like, the virtual and the real.

I very much doubt that our grandchildren will understand the distinction between that which is a computer and that which isn't.

Or, to put it another way, they will not know "computers" as any distinct category of object or function. This, I think, is the logical outcome of genuinely ubiquitous computing: the wired world. The wired world will consist, in effect, of a single unbroken interface. The idea of a device that "only" computes will perhaps be the ultimate archaism in a world in which the fridge or the toothbrush are potentially as smart as any other object, including you. A world in which intelligent objects communicate, routinely and constantly, with each other and with us. In this world, there will be no need for the physical augmentation of the human brain, as the most significant, and quite unthinkably powerful, augmentation will have already taken place postgeographically, via distributed processing.

You won't need smart goo in your brain, because your fridge and your toothbrush will be very smart indeed, enormously smart, and they will be there for you, constantly and always.

So it won't, I don't think, be a matter of computers crawling buglike down into the most intimate chasms of our being, but of humanity crawling buglike out into the dappled light and shadow of the presence of that which we will have created, which we are creating now, and which seems to me to already be in process of re-creating us.

This was an attempt to as literally and as thoroughly as possible answer the sort of question which I had, by this point, been asked many, many, many times.

I'm glad that we continue to be, for the most part, products of unskilled labor.

WILLIAM GIBSON'S FILMLESS FESTIVAL

WIRED
OCTOBER 1999

BUILT IN THE LATE TWENTIES heyday of the early studios, the Château Marmont boasts a fine deep mulch of Hollywood psychogeography, a wealth of ghosts. It's hard to imagine doing anything in one of these bungalows that someone hasn't already done, but maybe we're doing it tonight: We're holding our own private festival of digital video, screening films that were shot without the benefit of, well, film.

First up: *Dancehall Queen*, a feature from Jamaica that we'll watch with its co-writer and editor, Suzanne Fenn.

Suzanne was a member of Jean-Luc Godard's Dziga Vertov Group, circa 1970–71, where she functioned as the embodiment of Liberated Woman. Trained by the great documentary filmmaker Joris Ivens, she cut Errol Morris's *Gates of Heaven*, all of Michael Tolkin's movies, and films by Percy Adlon, Louis Malle, and many more.

Dancehall Queen, shot in the Jamaican ghetto of Standpipe, is an all-digital production, the result of Chris Blackwell's initial moves toward creating a modern movie studio/industry in Jamaica, based on the way digital cameras and editing pare down and open up the filmmaking process. That is, the way they reduce costs to a point where films can be feasibly geared to smaller audiences, thus allowing the development of true indigenous cinemas. It's the third-world version of what Americans call "guerrilla filmmaking," extending the same vocabulary of techniques and strategies: on-the-fly street shooting, more non-professional actors, and so forth.

What becomes apparent, listening to Suzanne and then watching her film, is that *Dancehall Queen* couldn't have been made without this technology. In a milieu of ambient squatters, working with conventional equipment and a large crew is virtually impossible. (There aren't even any viable authority figures to bribe.) The technology opens up the world in a new and global way: If you can go there, you can shoot there. For all her Euro-film pedigree, Suzanne is not the type to be held back by nostalgia for an old media platform, and *Dancehall Queen* uses the new technology to great effect, plunging the viewer into the outrageous color, hypnotic energy, and desperate socioeconomics of the Standpipe ghetto and its club scene.

As the film ends I glance over at my daughter Claire, 16, and see that she's excited, too, even though the movie's dialog is in a variant of English that would send American video distributors running to the nearest subtitle house.

Suzanne tells us that her next feature, also shot digitally in Jamaica, is called *Third World Cop*. I tell her that's the best title I've heard this year, and then we slot our second film, Hal Hartley's *The Book of Life*. Featuring singer P. J. Harvey as Jesus Christ's backpack-toting personal assistant, it was shot in Manhattan for French television on the proverbial shoestring.

On the final day of 1999, an immaculately suited Jesus and a

Bukowskiesque Devil warily circle each other through a series of sleazy bars and chilly law offices, trying to cut a deal that centers on Christ's PowerBook. This contains the biblical Seventh Seal: Unlock the file and the Judgment Day program will launch, and then all hell will break loose. Christ also unexpectedly finds himself on a quixotic last-minute mission to save the soul of a saintly waitress who has run afoul of the Devil's negotiating skills. The film displays a fine nervous energy, heightened by loose-limbed camerawork, Hartley seeming to relish the so-called limits of digital filmmaking: His images smear, blur, judder, pixelate, and twist. It's a weirdly compelling grammar he assembles, and the film is funny, tender, and vertiginous.

I check Claire again. I'm using her as a tunnel canary, those birds that miners employed to warn them of poisonous gases. If she goes comatose, we're definitely off the track in terms of a crucial target demographic. Will this stripped-down mode of production hold the attention of a teenager raised on studio product?

It looks as though Hartley's grabbed her, handheld and all, so now we're ready for Thomas Vinterberg's *The Celebration*, a Danish film, digitally shot, that won the Jury Prize last year at Cannes.

Vinterberg was proud to put *The Celebration* forward as an example of the principles codified in Dogma 95, a manifesto calling for location sound, natural lighting, and other new realities of digital filmmaking. The movie, staged in a very large and handsome chateau, explores the inner psychic recesses of the deeply troubled annual reunion of a very large and extraordinarily dysfunctional Danish family, and it seems . . . very long. After twenty minutes of Danish gloom I look over and see the tunnel-canary effect kicking in, big time. Claire's about to opt for bed and a head-clearing hit of MTV.

The Celebration is triggering my own Joe Bob Briggs reflex, but maybe that's because watching a triple feature is pushing it for me. Or maybe it's because the movie is 105 serious minutes of what *Variety* calls "arthouse," fraught with incest and repressed memories of child abuse. It definitely would've been a tough pitch in Burbank.

Still, though I may not be enjoying it tremendously, I can honestly be glad it exists. Vinterberg has probably made exactly the film he wanted to make—a lot of it, at that—and any technology that empowers this uniquely personal process is ultimately going to do some good.

So Claire goes to bed, *The Celebration* ends, Suzanne and my friend Roger depart, and I go out to the patio to smell the eucalyptus and think about dreams and platforms and how platforms affect dreams and vice versa.

Digital video strikes me as a new platform wrapped in the language and mythology of an old platform. Lamb dressed as mutton, somewhat in the way we think of our cellular systems as adjuncts of copper-wire telephony. The way we still "dial" on touchpads. We call movies "film," but the celluloid's drying up. Film today is already in a sense digital, since it's all edited using an Avid.

But people still come to Hollywood, and I know that some of the people driving the cars I can hear now, out on Sunset, desperately want to make movies. As I turn in, I think of the Garage Kubrick and wonder what he'd make of the films we've just seen. Probably not much.

The Garage Kubrick (he never quite managed to be assigned a name) is a character who somehow escaped the focus of my latest novel. He was there in the notes, but he didn't make it to the literary equivalent of the screen. He had already demonstrated his unwillingness to take his place in my book when I learned of Stanley Kubrick's death. The character was based not on Kubrick himself but on certain theories about Kubrick's methods and intentions that were put forward by a friend of mine, a young British director who once worked for him. Kubrick, my friend opined, didn't care how long anything took, and would have been happiest if he'd been able to construct virtual sets and virtual actors from the wireframe up. The idea took root in my college-film-history recollections of auteur theory—which has it that the director is, absolutely, the "author" of a given film, just as the writer is the author of a book.

Whether this is literally true is arguable, but the world, in my experience, is filled with wannabe auteurs, and my imagination conjured one particularly focused and obsessive example.

I thought of the Garage Kubrick when I went to Sundance for the first time and saw young filmmakers doing what young filmmakers apparently must do to get attention for their work—the public part of which seemed to involve shuffling in a tense sort of lemming-lockstep up and down the main drag of Park City, talking on two cell phones at once and looking near-fatally stressed. The private part, the deal-making part, I assumed (based on experiences of my own) would be worse. Or simply wouldn't happen.

Watching the Sundancers cultivate cell-phone tumors induced a certain empathy. I felt for these people. And that feeling fueled my fantasy of the Garage Kubrick.

Who is maybe fourteen, fifteen at most, and is either the last or the very first auteur—depending on how you look at it.

The Garage Kubrick hates everything that Sundance, let alone Hollywood, puts people through, and he won't have Slamdance or Slumdance either, or any of the rest of it.

The Garage Kubrick is a stone auteur, an adolescent near-future Orson Welles, plugged into some unthinkable (but affordable) node of consumer tech in his parents' garage. The Garage Kubrick is single-handedly making a feature in there, some sort of apparently live-action epic that may or may not involve motion capture. That may or may not involve human actors, but which will seem to.

The Garage Kubrick is a control freak to an extent impossible any further back along the technological timeline. He is making, literally, a one-man movie; he is his film's author to the degree that I had always assumed any auteur would want to be.

And he will not, consequently, come out of the garage. His parents, worried at first, have gone into denial. He is simply in there, making his film. Doing it the way my friend assumed Stanley Kubrick would have done it if he'd had the tech wherewithal.

And this, come to think of it, may be why the Garage Kubrick never made it into my book; I was never able to imagine him letting go of the act of creation long enough to emerge and interact with any other characters. But characters who miss the bus have a way of haunting their authors, and now, falling asleep at the Marmont, it comes to me: He's back, and I'm going to have to figure out where he fits in with this new technology. And whether or not we can, or if we'll want to, get there—where I've imagined him—from here.

We start the next day with blueberry pancakes and a couple of compilation tapes of digital short subjects, animations in one style or another, that remind me of Siggraph demos. The Garage Kubrick would recognize these, I suppose, as units in the language in which he's learning to sing opera.

At this point, Claire's real-life media needs start to manifest. She needs digital, but not film. She needs Japan-only PlayStation games and Final Fantasy associational items. We get on the road to Monrovia, where she's found the physical retail locus of a website called Game Cave. Game Cave turns out to be a much slicker, more contemporary operation than the fanboy pod-mall outlet I'd imagined, and while Claire makes her selections I consider that this place, rather than anything more conventionally cinematic, is where the Garage Kubrick is likely to emerge.

Maybe an entire culture of these people will emerge, since building digital sets from scratch might prove too difficult for most individuals. Maybe a specialist market selling things like templates for an American suburb, or mall interiors, or car chases. These could then be tweaked into more specific shapes by the individual enthusiast. Some people might find that their most valuable asset is the set they've developed, which they can rent to others, to modify, layer over, cut, paste, and sample.

Which has me scratching my head in Game Cave, as the concept is so strangely like aspects of contemporary Hollywood: an "industry" on the Net.

The Garage Kubrick mutters at me, wipes his sweaty hands on his dirty chinos, and goes back into the garage. He doesn't want this. He's the Author.

Back at the Marmont, we're watching 20 Dates, a film by Myles Berkowitz. "There's the place where we bought the Austin Powers teeth!" Claire says, delighted.

20 Dates was shot, more or less, in this neighborhood, so we score a very localized kind of déjà vu, an inverse vérité. We sit here, watching video of places a few blocks away, and feel— pleasurably—less real.

20 Dates cost around $65,000. With its Candid Camera aesthetic, it feels more like television than the other features we've screened, but in some ways it seems more radically itself. We watch the director tape his way through his twenty dates, looking for true love. Which he eventually, against serious odds, claims to find, so that in the end 20 Dates somehow feels a lot like the Hollywood product it tells us it's trying not to be.

Still, Myles made his movie and has an audience, so we chalk up one more to digital.

I suspect the Garage Kubrick was probably assigned projects like 20 Dates in fifth grade: Go out and make a film about your neighborhood, about people, about how you feel about girls, whatever. He did, but he hated doing it. He already knew what he wanted: high narrative tension, great sets, unforgettable characters, the texture of his own imagination turned into pixelflesh. He wanted the garage, that fertile darkness, unspeakable embrace with whatever artifact of convergence waited for him there.

Next up, after a lunch break, is Bennett Miller's *The Cruise*, a black-and-white documentary from New York that has attracted a sizable audience. This interests me more than it does the tunnel canary, who opts for the pool. I sink into the world of Timothy "Speed" Levitch, a tour guide on Gray Line buses, who looks a bit like the late John Lennon and can be almost as irritating as Myles Berkowitz. This is one of those idiosyncratic films about an idiosyncratic guy in what is still, in spite of everything, a pretty idiosyncratic city. I'm a fan of this sort of thing, and if there were a channel that ran such films all day— like Real One in my current novel—I'd surf it. *The Cruise* is, as they say in festival brochures, a very personal film, and very personal films are notoriously difficult to fund. If digital were any more expensive or any more technically demanding, these images probably wouldn't be here.

What do the films we've been watching have in common? A technology that facilitates motion capture and assembly, and does indeed put the tools of production into the hands of just about anyone with a serious hankering to make a film. But that's a simple observation, rather like saying that anyone with Microsoft Word can produce a book that looks, well, exactly like a book.

"Digital is an inexpensive way to make films," my friend Roger decides, as we watch the onedotzero3 cassette, a compilation from a recent digital-film festival at London's Institute of Contemporary Arts, "but it's a very expensive way to do club graffiti."

We've come out to Roger's place to access his multiformat VCR, our English tape being in PAL, but now there's a problem with the tape, or with the VCR, or with how the two interact: The imagery, a lot of which resembles clip art, is in black and white. It's supposed to be in color.

I feel guilty watching it this way. This is grossly unfair to the filmmakers, although it does seem to underline the idea that most of what we are watching here has been created either as a background for serious clubbing or as neurologically specific tools for the appreciation of proscribed substances, or both. If we could crank these images up to wall size, with full Dolby, I'm sure they'd jangle a few synapses. But largely abstract content, in monochrome, on a standard-size monitor, is simply an exercise in design.

The tunnel canary isn't comatose, but she's not watching, either. She's teaching herself to juggle with three large lemons from the tree in Roger's front yard.

Sleep eludes me. The Garage Kubrick is muttering, keeping me awake. Does anybody really need him? Will he ever happen?

I remember the people I've heard complain about the very texture of digital images, filmless film: how it lacks richness, depth. I've heard the same thing said about CDs. Someone once told me that it was Mark Twain who turned in the first typewritten manuscript, and this was generally thought to be a Bad

Thing: Work composed on a machine would naturally lack richness, depth.

But surely, says a very American part of me, things (if not people) can get better, and what the early stages of one technology take away can be restored in a later stage, or by a newer technology piggybacking on the first.

And my Garage Kubrick wants full fractal richness. He wants to control the very texture of the dream, down into its finest grain, its tightest resolution. He wants to build his characters from the ground up, from the inside out. He thinks not in terms of actors but in terms of models for motion capture. His medium is entirely plastic, to a degree that has never been possible before. And isn't, I remind myself, possible today.

But it might be eventually. It seems to me, really, that it must be one day.

Digital cinema has the potential to throw open the process of filmmaking, to make the act more universally available, to demythologize it, to show us aspects of the world we've not seen before. In that sense, it will be the "eyes" of the extended nervous system we've been extruding as a species for the past century.

To think in terms of entertainment, or even of art, is probably to miss the point. We are building ourselves mirrors that remember—public mirrors that wander around and remember what they've seen. That is a basic magic.

But a more basic magic still, and an older one, is the painting of images on the walls of caves, and in that magic the mind of the painter is the mirror, whatever funhouse twists are brought to the remembered object. And that cave is also my Kubrick's garage, and whatever he's driven to cook up in there will simply be another human dream. The real mystery lies in why he is, why we are, willing, driven, to do that.

Some of us will use digital film technology to explore all of those places, all of those people, in the world we're still trying to discover. If the Standpipes of the world cease thereby to be invisible, out of sight and out of mind, it will have all been worth it right there.

And others, like my own Garage Kubrick, will use the same technology to burrow more deeply, more obsessively, more gloriously, into the insoluble mystery of the self, even as the Château Marmont outlasts the media platform and the studio system that gave it birth.

I fall asleep imagining someone building a virtual Marmont, and in one of the bungalows, a character is falling asleep. . . .

My novel Pattern Recognition *was gestating, as I wrote this, the "Garage Kubrick" morphing from protagonist (or antagonist, or possibly just agonist) to MacGuffin, though I didn't know it.* Pattern Recognition *would eventually manage to be published just ahead of the launch of YouTube, a very good thing considering certain of its plot points.*

In a world with YouTube, it's probably much more difficult to induce a magazine to put you up in the Marmont to watch digital films, so that was good timing as well.

Over a decade later, digital cinema seems to be going where I thought it would, though with the paradoxical problem that lack of broad theatrical release is still taken to mean that your film didn't really happen. Unevenly distributed future, that; the towering edges of the footprint of the previous media platform . . . I imagine the true Kubricks to be going about their business regardless.

JOHNNY: NOTES ON A PROCESS

WIRED
JULY 1995

A CLEAR COLD Monday midmorning in Toronto, February 1994, and I'm standing beneath the dim high ceiling of a brick Victorian factory on Lansdowne Avenue, perhaps a foundry once for steam engines, more recently a General Electric plant. This room is vast, and in it are built other rooms, ceilingless, lights slung above. Here's a hotel suite, Beijing, early twenty-first century, realized in the most fastidious detail (though the faux Philippe Starck chairs have recently been riddled with explosive fléchettes, setting goose down to play across the wonderfully ugly carpet). Here's the back room of the Drome bar, with grease-stained ductwork to rival Gilliam's *Brazil*. And here, in a propman's plastic Ziploc bag, looking like a cross between some fetish queen's jewelry and the business end of a Roto-Rooter, is a weapon of a sort that has never before existed anywhere in the human universe. Except, that is, behind my forehead. Why we spent however many mornings driving to Century City in some rented car, with the windows down and the air-conditioning on, as if, thereby, we were stealing something from this system that so effortlessly, so seamlessly, so consistently refuses us . . .

I've become an intimate of Sunset Strip hotels, moving over these four years from Bel Age to Le Reve to the St. James, and finally to the Château Marmont, that historied pile, where the ghosts of Jim Morrison and Gram Parsons (who didn't actually die there, though they certainly served their time) sit around the pool at night with the ghost of John Belushi (who did). There I learned to stay in the "9" suites: 39, 49, 59, 69. These have balconies running the length of the building, facing the Strip, and more rooms than you can ever quite discover during a given stay. Like vast 1920s Hollywood apartments, their original fixtures and fittings strangely intact. Huge white gas ranges, deactivated dumbwaiters, cedar-lined closets with fold-down ironing boards. A place fraught with mysteries. Mysteries and intriguing-looking European tourists, who stand around the front desk complaining of irregularities in their wives' rented cellular service. Complaining of strange voices, speaking as from the very well of time. Of a madman on Frau X's pocket Motorola, muttering that the severed finger joint of one particular and long-forgotten Fifties starlet languishes this very day in the locked drawer of that odd brown piece of furniture in the hallway of Suite Sixtysomething—but the precise location is always lost, awash in that ferocious garble of Russian cab-static, up off the crawling Strip, where the cabbies, mainly Vietnamese when I began my term of service (four years ago? five?) are now mostly from Vladivostok.

Not to say that I wasn't happier at the Marmont, once I discovered the place. My home away from home. Glitz-free. Patient to a fault, the Marmont. A place proud of its Bohemian heritage.

A place to sit up late at night, rereading whatever current draft, so curiously indistinguishable from the last, while pondering what it might be, exactly, that one does in order to make this strange thing, a movie, happen? And they do happen, movies, because through the window, past the palms and the shadow of the Marlboro Man, you can see the billboards down Sunset, the ones announcing all the new films. Yes, but movies are quite impossible to make. Utterly. It cannot be done. And yet. And yet . . . So that life, or anyway the segments of it concerned with trying to make this movie, becomes a sort of Kafka loop, but Kafka as done by the Fox Network, say. So that you go away. Go home. Back to the world. But eventually it tugs you back yet again, as if on a bungee made of prepaid first-class air tickets and something that starts to feel, well, fairly deeply compulsive—yes, even a mania of sorts . . . To cut the Kafka-loop bits short, what initially sounds like yes, but—no no no no no begins to sound like yes, of course, but no no no no, and, well, yes—except of course when we mean no.

When it's virtually all yes, you find several million dollars at your project's disposal (though quite amazingly useless, you discover, and which, anyway, under no circumstances whatever, including any eventual making of the film, will ever belong to you) but the rare no really means it, and while that no is there, some eldritch entity in Dimension Zed, be it a faceless Bahamian banker, her cousin the Parisian tax lawyer, an Alaskan accountant, or Herr Virek in his designer cancer-vat in Neo Zurich (and believe me, you'll never know) will not sign the check you need to secure "the talent"—i.e., "name" actors—without whom you cannot make this movie. And it goes on like that. And, well, on.

So that, sadly, when at last you are flushed through that very final membrane, you scarcely even know it. You are, in some odd and I suppose merciful way, past caring. It's all very odd. You're kind of like one of those hapless yet endearingly tough-talking personality-constructs in a William Gibson novel. The part of you that is most nearly human has come to inhabit certain interstices in a piece of software called "scriptor." You have started to experience everything in terms of Scriptor's "Work". menu. When you enter a room, you feel a momentary anxiety: Should this be under "scene" heading, or "action"? You aren't sure, so you say something, really anything, to the first person you see, because that will definitely be under "dialog." You have been working fourteen-hour days, six-day weeks, for the past two months. Your family, when they see you, look at you oddly. You dream of having a personal assistant. Someone to handle all the little things, like relating to your children and brushing your teeth. You experience moments of terrible lucidity, in which you see how deeply and cosmically silly this whole experience has gotten to be. Meanwhile, your friend who wants to be a director has relocated to Toronto, where the "film"—you've taken to thinking of it in quotation marks—is supposedly to be shot. He has taken his pregnant wife, their two children from a previous marriage, into the bitterest, most nightmarish winter in Canadian history. And he has already spent literally millions of somebody's dollars on . . . something. You aren't quite sure what. And the check has not been signed. Not quite. No.

And then they sign it. And the director—and now he is the director—begins to shoot. Things begin to move at a really frantic pace. Because now there is the relentless logic of fitting a hundred and five suddenly very intricate pages of story into only fifty-six days of shooting. Meanwhile the talent has been signed as well. Actors have arrived to inhabit these creatures of your imagination. It's all very strange. Deeply strange. People with walkie-talkies. Cars and drivers. Catering vans. The leading lady is off behind the Beijing Hotel set, teaching herself to peg ninja-spikes into a sheet of Styrofoam. People from the Smoke-Wafters Union are wafting prop smoke into the back room of the Drome bar. Things are beginning to move. It's happening.

The actor who plays Yomomma, the transsexual bodyguard, asks you if his character has a penis. You tell him quite frankly that nobody knows except Pretty, his girlfriend. Who else, after all, would dare to ask? He seems to like that.

Then you go away, and you talk about all this too much, boring your family, your friends, with your monotonous obsession. You show them the photographs you've taken. They shrug. You make an effort to behave normally. It doesn't work. You're not sure what to do. So you go back to Toronto to look at the Beijing Hotel suite again—and it's gone forever, dismantled. As is the back room of the Drome bar.

You find all that's left of the hotel suite—a filthy stretch of carpeting and a shredded fake Philippe Starck chair—in an even bigger building out in the suburban industrial belt. An address on Industry Street, a disused transformer factory. Someone's painted "pcb's 'r' us" over the door to the soundstage. Here the director and the production designer have caused to be constructed the mother of all garbage constructs, something really huge, big *gomi*, like a section of the bridge in *Virtual Light*, a demented, heartbreakingly lyrical, 3D collage of cargo containers, dumpsters, an Airstream trailer, a cabin cruiser, a school bus. And you walk out on it, into it, as strange winds of time and art and possibility blow through you, and you remember reading the City of Interzone section in *Naked Lunch* when you were fourteen years old, for the very first time. And this is it. And you aren't crying, but you know that it's very possible you might. . . .

And then, then suddenly, it all reverses itself, swings around, back into the real world and you know that it will never be that for you again, be real or almost, but that's okay. You were there, finally, if only for a very fleeting instant, and now you can actually go back to the real world and talk to your own children and maybe even brush your own teeth.

You don't have to do this anymore.

(Except that there's something called "post production," and they haven't really told you about that yet.)

My innocence, at the time writing the above, ignorant not only of post-production but of many other things, was actually quite complete. I had, mercifully, absolutely no idea. I'm very glad of having written this, though, as it serves today to remind me that the process was not without its own very peculiar pleasures.

GOOGLING THE CYBORG

TALK FOR THE VANCOUVER INSTITUTE

FEBRUARY 2008

THE FIRST INTIMATIONS of the cyborg, for me, were the robots in a 1940 Republic serial called *The Mysterious Dr. Satan*. These robots had been recycled from the earlier *Undersea Kingdom*, 1936, and would appear again in the brilliantly titled *Zombies of the Stratosphere*, 1952. I have those dates and titles not because I'm any sort of expert on Republic serials, or even on science fiction in general, but because I've bookmarked Google. But we'll get back to Google later.

The Mysterious Dr. Satan was among my earliest cinematic experiences. I probably saw it in 1952, and I definitely saw it on a television whose cabinet was made out of actual wood, something that strikes me today as wholly fantastic. These Republic cliffhangers, made originally for theatrical release, one episode at a time, were recycled in the Fifties for local broadcast in the after-school slot, after half an hour of black-and-white Hollywood cartoons.

I can remember being utterly terrified by Dr. Satan's robots, which had massive tubular bodies, no shoulders, hands like giant Vise-Grip pliers, and limbs made of some sort of flexible metal tubing. They had been on the job since 1936, which contributed strongly to the weirdness of their design language, but I had no way of knowing that. I just knew that they were the scariest thing I'd ever seen, and I could barely stand to watch them menace the hero or his girlfriend.

I wonder now what I knew about robots. That they were called "robots," and were "mechanical men." That these particular robots were the servants of Dr. Satan. Did I believe that they were autonomous, or that Dr. Satan controlled them? Probably the latter, as menacing-robot scenes in serials of this sort often involved a sort of telepresence, and the suggestion of remote control. Cut from robot, menacing, to evil scientist in his lab, watching robot menace on television screen. Evil scientist closes giant knife-switch, which causes robot to menace even harder.

Given that I was watching this material in the early Fifties, I would shortly become familiar with the expression "electronic brain," which like "rocket ship" was there as a marker of something anticipated but not yet here. Actually, it already was here, and had been since World War II, but most people didn't know it yet. And that is where postwar science fiction, in retrospect, got it most broadly wrong: All eyes were on the rocket ship, relatively few on the electronic brain. We all know, today, which one's had the greater impact.

An electronic brain. What would you do with one of those, if you had one? In 1940, you'd probably stick it in a machine of some kind. Not one of Dr. Satan's recycled Atlantean robots, but something practical. In, say, a machine that could weld leaf-springs in a Milwaukee tractor factory.

This is about what science-fiction writers call "Steam Engine Time." The observable fact that steam, contained, exerts force, has been around since the first lid rattled as the soup came to a boil. The ancient Greeks built toy steam engines that whirled bronze globes. But you won't get a locomotive till it's Steam Engine Time.

What you wouldn't do, in 1940, with an electronic brain, would be to stick it on your desk, connect it somehow to a typewriter, and, if you, had one, a television of the sort demonstrated at the 1939 World's Fair in New York. At which point it would start to resemble . . . But it's not Steam Engine Time yet, so you can't do that. Although you would, or anyway you'd think about it, if you were a man named Vannevar Bush, but we'll come back to him later. Vannevar Bush almost single-handedly invented what we now think of as the military-industrial complex. He did that for Franklin Roosevelt, but it isn't what he'll be remembered for.

I can't remember a robot ever scaring me that much, after Dr. Satan's robots. They continued to be part of the cultural baggage of sci-fi, but generally seemed rather neutral, at least to me. Good or bad depending on who was employing them in a given narrative. Isaac Asimov wrote a whole shelf of novels working out a set of hardwired ethics for intelligent robots, but I never got into them. The tin guys didn't, by the Sixties, seem to me to be what was interesting in science fiction, and neither did spaceships. It was what made Asimov's robots intelligent in the first place that would have interested me, had I thought of it, but I didn't.

Steam Engine Time, again. What interested me most in the sci-fi of the Sixties was the investigation of the politics of perception, some of which, I imagine, could now be seen in retrospect as having been approached through various and variously evolving ideas of the cyborg. Stories about intelligent rocket ships and how humans might interact with them, or stories of humans forced through circumstances to become the nonelectronic brain in an otherwise traditional robot. A sort of projection was under way, an exploration of boundaries. And meanwhile, out in the world, the cyborg was arriving. Or continuing to arrive.

Though not in science fiction's sense of the cyborg, which was that of a literal and specific human-machine hybrid. There's a species of literalism in our civilization that tends to infect science fiction as well: It's easier to depict the union of human and machine literally, close-up on the cranial jack please, than to describe the true and daily and largely invisible nature of an all-encompassing embrace.

The real cyborg, cybernetic organism in the broader sense, had been busy arriving as I watched Dr. Satan on that wooden television in 1952. I was becoming a part of something, in the act of watching that screen. We all were. We are today. The human species was already in the process of growing itself an extended communal nervous system, and was doing things with it that had previously been impossible: viewing things at a distance, viewing things that had happened in the past, watching dead men talk and hearing their words. What had been absolute limits of the experiential world had in a very real and literal way been profoundly and amazingly altered, extended, changed. And would continue to be. And the real marvel of this was how utterly we took it all for granted.

Science fiction's cyborg was a literal chimera of meat and machine. The world's cyborg was an extended human nervous system: film, radio, broadcast television, and a shift in perception so profound that I believe we've yet to understand it. Watching television, we each became aspects of an electronic brain. We became augmented. In the Eighties, when Virtual Reality was the buzzword, we were presented with images of . . . television! If the content is sufficiently engrossing, however, you don't need wraparound deep-immersion goggles to shut out the world. You grow your own. You are there. Watching the content you most want to see, you see nothing else.

The physical union of human and machine, long dreaded and long anticipated, has been an accomplished fact for decades, though we tend not to see it. We tend not to see it because we are it, and because we still employ Newtonian paradigms that tell us that "physical" has only to do with what we can see, or touch. Which of course is not the case. The electrons streaming into a child's eye from the screen of the wooden television are as physical as anything else. As physical as the neurons subsequently moving along that child's optic nerves. As physical as the structures and chemicals those neurons will encounter in the human brain. We are implicit, here, all of us, in a vast physical construct of artificially linked nervous systems. Invisible. We cannot touch it.

We are it. We are already the Borg, but we seem to need myth to bring us to that knowledge.

Steam Engine Time. Somewhere in the late Seventies. In garages, in California. Putting the electronic brain on the table. Doing an end run around Dr. Asimov's ethical robots. The arms and legs, should you require them, are mere peripherals. To any informed contemporary child, a robot is simply a computer being carried around by its peripherals. Actually I think this accounts for the generally poor sales of several recent generations of commercial humanoid robots; they're all more than a little embarrassing, at some level. Sony's Aibo, a robot dog, does slightly better in the market. Who today wouldn't simply prefer to have a faster and more powerful computer, faster Internet access? That's where the action is. That augmentation. Of the user. Of us.

Actually, the return of those humanoid robots has disappointed me. I'd thought that everyone had gotten it: that you don't need to go anthropocentric in order to get work done. That in fact you get far less work done, far less bang for your buck, if you do. My idea of an efficient robot today would be an American Predator drone with Hellfire missiles, or one of the fly-sized equivalents allegedly on Pentagon CAD-CAM screens, if not already in the field. Though actually those are both cyborgs, or borg-aspects, as they are capable both of autonomous actions and actions via telepresent control. When the human operator uplinks, operator and Predator constitute a cyborg. A friend of mine wrote a short story, a decade ago, in which the protagonists were Soviet equivalents of Predator drones, but literal cyborgs: small fighter aircraft controlled by brain-in-bottle onboard pilots, with very little left in the way of bodies. But why, today, bother building those? (Unless of course to provide the thrill of piloting to someone who might otherwise not experience it, which would be a worthy goal in my view.) But for purely military purposes, without that live meat on board, aircraft are capable of executing maneuvers at speeds that would kill a human being. The next generation of U.S. fighter aircraft, for this and other tactical reasons, will almost certainly be physically unmanned.

Martian jet lag. That's what you get when you operate one of those little Radio Shack wagon/probes from a comfortable seat back at an airbase in California. Literally. Those operators were the first humans to experience Martian jet lag. In my sense of things, we should know their names: first humans on the Red Planet. Robbed of recognition by that same old school of human literalism.

This is the sort of thing that science fiction, traditionally, is neither good at predicting, nor, should we predict it, at describing.

Vannevar Bush, whom I mentioned earlier, was not a science-fiction writer. In World War II he was chief scientific adviser to Franklin Roosevelt, and director of the Office of Scientific Research and Development, where he supervised the work that led to the creation of the atomic bomb. He more or less invented the military-industrial complex, as we call it today. In 1945, he published an article in *The Atlantic Monthly* titled, "As We May Think." In this article he imagined a system he called the "memex," short for "memory extender." If there was a more eerily prescient piece of prose, fiction or otherwise, written in the first half the twentieth century, I don't know it.

This article is remembered most often, today, for having first envisioned what we call the principle of "hyperlinking," a means of connecting disparate but conceptually involved units of data. But I've never read it that way, myself. I think Vannevar Bush envisioned the cyborg, in the sense I've been suggesting we most valuably use that word.

One remarkable thing about this is that he seemed to have no particular idea that electronics would have anything to do with it. He begins by imagining an engineer, a technocrat figure, equipped with a "walnut-sized" (his phrase) camera, which is strapped to the center of his forehead, its shutter operated by a handheld remote. The technocrat's glasses are engraved with crosshairs. If he can see it, he can photograph it.

Bush imagines this as a sort of pre-Polaroid microfilm device, "dry photography" he calls it, and he imagines his technocrat snapping away at project sites, blueprints, documents, as he works.

He then imagines the memex itself, a desk (oak, he actually suggests, reminding me of my television set in 1952) with frosted glass screens inset in its top, on which the user can call up those images previously snapped with that forehead-walnut. Also in the desk are all of the user's papers, business records, etc., all stored as instantly retrievable microfiche, plus the contents of whole specialized libraries.

At this point, Bush introduces the idea which earns him his

place in conventional histories of computing: the idea of somehow marking "trails" through the data, a way of navigating, of being able to backtrack. The hyperlink idea.

But what I see, when I look at Bush's engineer, with his Polaroid walnut and his frosted-glass, oak-framed desktop, is the cyborg. In both senses. A creature of Augmented rather than Virtual Reality. He is . . . us! As close to the reality of being us, today, as anyone in 1945 (or perhaps in 1965, for that matter) ever managed to get! Bush didn't have the technology to put beneath the desktop, so he made do with what he knew, but he's describing the personal computer. He's describing, with an accuracy of prediction that still gives me goose bumps, how these devices will be used. How the user's memory will be augmented, and connected to whole Borgesian libraries, searchable and waiting. Google! The memex, awaiting the engineer's search-string!

But in our future, awaiting the interconnectedness of desktops. Awaiting the Net. Bush didn't see that, that we'd link memexes, and create libraries in common. Steam Engine Time: He couldn't go there, though he got closer than anyone else, in his day, to getting it.

There's my cybernetic organism: the Internet. If you accept that "physical" isn't only the things we can touch, it's the largest man-made object on the planet, or will be, soon: It's outstripping the telephone system, or ingesting it, as I speak. And we who participate in it are physically a part of it. The Borg we are becoming.

So for me the sci-fi cyborg, the meat/metal hybrid, is already another of those symbols, somewhat in the way that Dr. Satan's robots had their origin, as symbols, in a Czech satirist's view of alienated labor. The real deal is that which we already participate in daily, meld with, grow into.

The big news in biology this week was the announcement that we've stopped evolving, in the biological sense. I'll buy that. Technology has stopped us, and technology will take us on, into a new evolution, one Mr. Bush never dreamed of, and neither, I'm sure, have I.

Interface evolves toward transparency. The one you have to devote the least conscious effort to, survives, prospers. This is true for interface hardware as well, so that the cranial jacks and brain inserts and bolts in the neck, all the transitional sci-fi hardware of the sci-fi cyborg, already looks slightly quaint.

The real cyborg, the global organism, is so splendidly invasive that these things already seem medieval. They fascinate, much as torture instruments do, or reveal erotic possibilities to the adventurous, or beckon as stages or canvases for the artist, but I doubt that very many of us will ever go there. The real-deal cyborg will be deeper and more subtle and exist increasingly at the particle level, in a humanity where unaugmented reality will eventually be a hypothetical construct, something we can only try, with great difficulty, to imagine—as we might try, today, to imagine a world without electronic media.

This was for a series of evening lectures at the University of British Columbia. I decided to assume that the audience wouldn't necessarily be familiar with my fiction, and to try to explain, without announcing it, what I think my work tries to convey about technology.

That's the sort of thing journalists like to ask, and which I usually assume is impossible to answer, with any honesty or thoroughness. Sometimes it's good to have an excuse to be patient with oneself, and see where things go.

CREDITS

"African Thumb Piano" copyright © 2011 by William Gibson. Published here for the first time.

"Rocket Radio" copyright © 1989 by William Gibson. First published by *Rolling Stone* magazine, June 15, 1989.

"Since 1948" copyright © 2002 by William Gibson. First published by www.williamgibsonbooks.com, November 6, 2002.

"Any 'Mount of World" published without attribution at the original publisher's request.

"The Baddest Dude on Earth" copyright © 2002 by TimeAsia. First published by *Time International*, April 29, 2002. Published by arrangement with Time Inc.

"Talk for Book Expo, New York" speech delivered at Book Expo America, New York, May 27, 2010. Published here for the first time.

"Dead Man Sings" copyright © 1998 by William Gibson. First published by *Forbes ASAP* magazine, November 30, 1998.

"Up the Line" speech delivered at Directors Guild of America's Digital Day, Los Angeles, May 17, 2003. Published here for the first time.

"Disneyland with the Death Penalty" copyright © 1993 by William Gibson. First published by *Wired* magazine, January 2004.

"Mr. Buk's Window" copyright © 2001 by William Gibson. First published by www.williamgibsonbooks.com.

"Shiny Balls of Mud: *Hikaru Dorodango* and Tokyu Hands" copyright © 2002 by William Gibson. First published by *Tate* magazine, Issue 1, September/October 2002. Published by arrangement with Tate Publishing.

"An Invitation" copyright © 2007 by William Gibson. First published in *Labyrinths: Selected Stories and Other Writings* by Jorge Luis Borges. New York: New Directions Press, 2007.

"Metrophagy: The Art and Science of Digesting Great Cities" copyright © 2001 by William Gibson. First published by Whole Earth Catalog, Summer 2001. Published by arrangement with Bruce Sterling, editor.

"Modern Boys and Mobile Girls" copyright © 2001 by William Gibson. First published by *The Observer*, March 31, 2001.

"My Obsession" copyright © 1999 by William Gibson. First published by *Wired* magazine, January 1999.

"My Own Private Tokyo" copyright © 2001 by William Gibson. First published by *Wired* magazine, September 2001.

"The Road to Oceania" copyright © 2003 by William Gibson. First published by *The New York Times*, June 25, 2003.

"Skip Spence's Jeans" copyright © 2003 by *Ugly Things* magazine. Published by arrangement with *Ugly Things* magazine (first published by *Ugly Things* magazine, Issue 21).

"Terminal City," an introduction to *Phantom Shanghai* by Greg Girard, copyright © 2006 by The Magenta Foundation. Published by arrangement with The Magenta Foundation.

"Introduction: 'The Body'" from *Stelarc: The Monograph* by Marquard Smith, foreword by William Gibson. Cambridge, MA: The MIT Press, copyright © MIT 2005. Published by arrangement with MIT Press.

"The Net Is a Waste of Time" copyright © 1996 by William Gibson. First published by *The New York Times*, July 14, 1996.

"Time Machine Cuba" copyright © 2006 by William Gibson. First published in *The Infinite Matrix*, January 23, 2006. Published by arrangement with Eileen Gunn.

"Will We Have Computer Chips in Our Heads?" copyright © 2000 by William Gibson. Previously published as "Will We Plug Chips Into Our Brains?" by *Time* magazine, June 19, 2000.

"William Gibson's Filmless Festival" copyright © 1999 by William Gibson. First published by *Wired* magazine, October 1999.

"Johnny: Notes on a Process" copyright © 1995 by William Gibson. First published as "Remembering Johnny" by *Wired* magazine, October 1999.

"Googling the Cyborg" speech delivered at Vancouver Art Gallery, Vancouver, 2002. First published by www.williamgibsonbooks.com.